SUPERNATURAL
FINANCES

DESTINY IMAGE BOOKS BY DR. KEVIN L. ZADAI

Praying from the Heavenly Realms

The Agenda of Angels

SUPERNATURAL
FINANCES

HEAVEN'S BLUEPRINT FOR
BLESSING & INCREASE

KEVIN L. ZADAI

DESTINY IMAGE® PUBLISHERS, INC.

P.O. Box 310, Shippensburg, PA 17257-0310

"Promoting Inspired Lives."

This book and all other Destiny Image and Destiny Image Fiction books are available at Christian bookstores and distributors worldwide.

Cover design by Eileen Rockwell

Interior design by Terry Clifton

For more information on foreign distributors, call 717-532-3040.

Reach us on the Internet: www.destinyimage.com.

ISBN 13 TP: 978-0-7684-5135-1
ISBN 13 eBook: 978-0-7684-5136-8
ISBN 13 HC: 978-0-7684-5138-2
ISBN 13 LP: 978-0-7684-5137-5

For Worldwide Distribution, Printed in the U.S.A.

2 3 4 5 6 7 8 / 23 22 21 20 19

DEDICATION

I dedicate this book to the Lord Jesus Christ. When I died during surgery and met with Jesus on the other side, He insisted that I return to life on the earth and that I help people with their destinies. Because of Jesus's love and concern for people, the Lord has actually chosen to send a person back from death to help everyone who will receive that help so that his or her destiny and purpose is secure in Him. I want You, Lord, to know that when You come to take me to be with You someday, it is my sincere hope that people remember not me, but the revelation of Jesus Christ that You have revealed through me. I want others to know that I am merely being obedient to Your heavenly calling and mission, which is to reveal Your plan for the fulfillment of the divine destiny for each of God's children.

ACKNOWLEDGMENTS

In addition to sharing my story with everyone through the books *Heavenly Visitation: A Guide to the Supernatural, Days of Heaven on Earth: A Guide to the Days Ahead, A Meeting Place with God, Your Hidden Destiny Revealed, Praying from the Heavenly Realms: Supernatural Secrets to a Lifestyle of Answered Prayer,* and *The Agenda of Angels*, the Lord gave me a commission to produce this book, *Supernatural Finances*. This book addresses some of the revelations concerning the areas that Jesus reviewed and revealed to me through the Word of God and by the Spirit of God during several visitations. I want to thank everyone who has encouraged me, assisted me, and prayed for me during the writing of this work, especially my spiritual parents, Dr. Jesse Duplantis and Dr. Cathy Duplantis. Special thanks to my wonderful wife Kathi for her love and dedication to the Lord and to me. Thank you, Destiny Image and staff, for your support of this project. Thank you, Sid Roth and staff, for your love of our supernatural Messiah, Jesus. Thank you, Dr. Janet Kline, for the wonderful job editing this book. Special thanks, as well, to all my friends who know about Supernatural Finances and how the to operate in them for the next move of God's Spirit!

CONTENTS

INTRODUCTION

THROUGH KNOWLEDGE OF HIS WORD, IT IS POSSIBLE FOR every Christian to have a great understanding of the nature of the Lord and of His ways. I often wonder how some Christians appear to God Almighty when, without having learned of Him through His Word and while completely lacking crucial and essential understanding of Him, they try to interpret His ways. Without true knowledge of the Lord, knowledge that is easily accessed by reading of Him in the Bible, Christians often assume they do know Him when they have almost no understanding whatsoever of His ways.

God has graciously revealed Himself through His Word in many avenues. One way that He reveals Himself is through His spoken word. A second way that He reveals Himself is through His written Word. A third way that He reveals Himself is through His incarnate Word. When I met Jesus face to face, He clearly proved Himself to be complete in all three of these elements: He is the spoken Word, He is the written Word, and He is the incarnate Word. All three of these facets of the Word are encapsulated into one Person.

God has a strong personality. In every situation and in every circumstance, whatever our Father, the Holy Spirit, and Jesus have determined and agreed will always take precedence. The Holy Trinity will never be usurped or overtaken by anything other than what Jesus, the Father, and the Holy Ghost have agreed. The Trinity will never allow that to happen. God spoke all that was ever intended for mankind. And after He spoke those intents for mankind, He took care to ensure that His plan for mankind was written down. Therefore, He has taken great care to reveal His plan to His own in His Word. Christians need to avail themselves of the revelation within the Word so they begin to understand the Lord more completely.

Because man sinned and disobeyed God, we now live in a fallen world that needs a savior. Jesus came in the flesh to demonstrate the Father's personality toward us. That personality is one of the purest love that has ever existed. I am honestly at a loss for words to describe how mankind sometimes is so presumptuous as to judge God through the eyes of a fallen world. I am also at a loss for words to describe how mankind sometimes is so presumptuous to judge God through the eyes of the broken system of that fallen world. People continue to judge God in this way, completely oblivious to the fact that they do not have any correct understanding or any evidence of the ways of the Lord or even have basic informational truth concerning the Lord. The religious ideas of this fallen world create such a misrepresentation of the Lord. People often fail to realize the truth concerning the Lord that can be gained through knowledge of the Word of God.

When I met with Jesus, I told Him, face to face, that He was the most misrepresented Person on the earth. Most of mankind's perception of Him was not anything close to an accurate description of the true Savior who loves us far beyond what we could ever ask or think. I want to explain to everyone how much better Jesus is in reality than anyone could ever imagine. Jesus told me how the enemy tries to sidetrack people away from their God-given destiny. As He explained the strategies of the enemy that are meant to distract us from our eternal destinies, I began to realize the actual depth of how different Jesus is in truth from the Person whom most people perceive.

All of our destinies are written down in a book in Heaven. I saw that the Holy Spirit is sent to lead every one of us into all truth. Part of this truth is exceedingly important to our victory in life, and that part of truth that is essential to victory is this fact: God wants His people to prosper. It was easy to understand how the enemy does not want the revelation of prosperity to be readily received by Christians. If His children knew the importance of prosperity, according to the way the Lord has predetermined that prosperity come forth to ensure victory for His people in life, Christians would understand the vital need to have prosperity. They would begin to grasp the extent of how they are to control the wealth of the world. The control of the wealth of the world is essential for the Kingdom of God to accomplish its task to prepare the people of the earth for the Lord's second coming and to prepare them for the great end-time harvest of souls into God's Kingdom. Although the Gospel is free to all who will receive it, it takes great finances to spread the Good News of Jesus in the earth. People must go, and in going there are many costs, and one of the costs is financial.

Jesus showed me that the Spirit of God would begin to lead people into prosperity if they would yield to the will of God for their life. However, the yielding requires that one possess the right motive. The motive of pursuing the wealth just to obtain wealth is a corrupt goal. Financial prosperity for the Kingdom's sake is the goal that encompasses the right motive. Those who seek financial prosperity for the building of the Kingdom of God will reach the goal that the Lord set. However, those seeking financial wealth merely for obtaining wealth will not reach the goal that the Lord set. The Spirit of God desires to reach those without Christ in this world with the Good News of Jesus. He therefore very passionately desires to lead His people into the truth concerning *supernatural finances.*

When I met with Him, Jesus focused upon this truth: every Christian must permit the Holy Spirit to take the lead in his or her life. When Christians permit the Lord to freely lead them, they will definitely be led to enter into prosperity in every area of life. That prosperity will not only be prosperity that pertains to the area of money. Jesus wants every Christian to understand that He will never limit anyone; it is His desire that every Christian will fulfill his or her destiny in Him. Simply put, Jesus desires to finance this last great end-time harvest with unlimited supernatural provision from Heaven. Jesus plans to provide that unlimited supernatural provision from Heaven for anyone who can be trusted with wealth. Trusting those who will handle that wealth to support the last great revival on earth is part of the plan to prepare the earth before the Lord returns.

My personal recommendation is that every Christian learn of God's desire to place supernatural finances into his or her hands! If a Christian can pass this money test, then he or she will be ready to become an essential part of the end-time harvest. It is my desire that every Christian who desires to be a part of God's plan for this time on earth must take the necessary steps to become blessed with supernatural finances. Then, each Christian who seeks to become blessed with supernatural finances so that he or she can help to fund the final move of God will be eligible to join me in full participation for preparation for the end-time harvest before the return of our Lord to the earth!

—Dr. Kevin L. Zadai

Chapter 1

The Supernatural Advantage

God has a powerful Kingdom that is advancing. Remember, it is a spiritual Kingdom that manifests in this physical realm through what we call a *supernatural* event. We only need to have the Holy Spirit open our spiritual eyes to the activity of God's Kingdom business.

On the other hand, satan's kingdom is established and run by a spiritual entity that allowed rebellion to come into his heart. When this rebellion manifested in his life, he stole, by deception, the family that God Almighty had created called humanity.

You were the anointed cherub who covers; I established you; you were on the holy mountain of God; you walked back and forth in the midst of fiery stones. You were perfect in your ways from the day you were created, till iniquity was found in you. By the abundance of your trading you became filled with violence within, and you sinned; therefore I cast you as a profane thing out of the mountain of God; and I destroyed you, O covering cherub, from the midst of the fiery stones. Your heart was lifted up because of your beauty; you corrupted your wisdom for the sake of your splendor; I cast you to the ground, I laid you before kings, that they might gaze at you. You defiled your sanctuaries by the multitude of your iniquities, by the iniquity of your trading; therefore I brought fire from your midst; it devoured you, and I turned you to ashes upon the earth in the sight of all who saw you (Ezekiel 28:14-18).

FINDING A DIME

I remember when the Lord shared with me concerning the kingdom of darkness in this world. Jesus showed me how Lucifer became corrupted. He was initially called Helel (pronounced Hay-Lale; the word can be found in Strong's Concordance H1966 and is used in Isaiah 14:22). Helel means "shining one" or "son of the morning." Helel was translated into English as the name *lucifer*, which is not in the text of Isaiah. Helel was the name of this anointed cherub when God first created him. Lucifer is his current name that he received after his fall. Lucifer/Helel was cast out because of the *"abundance of your trading you became filled with violence within, and you sinned."*

When lucifer took over the earth after Adam fell, he was corrupt, and he enslaved man. The debt system we have today in the world is a direct result of this.

He does not want any of God's people to prosper in anything. Because of this corruption, he has made a system that is corrupt as well that keeps people enslaved or in extreme prosperity that keeps them away from depending wholly upon God. Because of his iniquity, he wants to keep control of this world by controlling the economic system of this earth.

It was lucifer's idea that a man/Christian must be poor unless he sells his soul to the devil and serves him. There is a false teaching circulating that it was God who did this to help man remain humble so that he would qualify to inherit the Kingdom of God and that Christians should not obtain any earthly possessions. This teaching is contrary to what God gave through a covenant to Abraham, Isaac, and Jacob, and the law of Moses. For instance, even tithing was instituted before the law of Moses, not when the law came into being, so that God's people could operate in the Kingdom of God.

Believe it or not, lucifer does not even want you to find a dime in the parking lot after church! Satan hates Christians and does not even want them to have a dime that they may have noticed in a church parking lot!

When a Christian finds a dime, satan considers this stealing from him. He will fight a Christian over any kind of increase except in the area of sin or any kind of evil. When you enter into *supernatural finances,* it is a direct result of being obedient to the Word of God. When you dedicate all that you have to God and then give a portion to support the preaching of the Gospel, you are going to participate in a supernatural event. According to a powerful passage of Scripture written by the apostle Paul in Second Corinthians 9, we are going to reap in the supernatural what we sow:

> *Now [remember] this: he who sows sparingly will also reap sparingly, and he who sows generously [that blessings may come to others] will also reap generously*

[and be blessed]. Let each one give [thoughtfully and with purpose] just as he has decided in his heart, not grudgingly or under compulsion, for God loves a cheerful giver [and delights in the one whose heart is in his gift]. And God is able to make all grace [every favor and earthly blessing] come in abundance to you, so that you may always [under all circumstances, regardless of the need] have complete sufficiency in everything [being completely self-sufficient in Him], and have an abundance for every good work and act of charity. As it is written and forever remains written, "He [the benevolent and generous person] scattered abroad, he gave to the poor, His righteousness endures forever!" Now He who provides seed for the sower and bread for food will provide and multiply your seed for sowing [that is, your resources] and increase the harvest of your righteousness [which shows itself in active goodness, kindness, and love]. You will be enriched in every way so that you may be generous, and this [generosity, administered] through us is producing thanksgiving to God [from those who benefit]. For the ministry of this service (offering) is not only supplying the needs of the saints (God's people), but is also overflowing through many expressions of thanksgiving to God. Because of this act of ministry, they will glorify God for your obedience to the gospel of Christ which you confess, as well as for your generous participation [in this gift] for them and for all [the other believers in need], and they also long for you while they pray on your behalf, because of the surpassing measure of God's

grace [His undeserved favor, mercy, and blessing which is revealed] in you. Now thanks be to God for His indescribable gift [which is precious beyond words]! (2 Corinthians 9:6-15 AMP)

ABUNDANCE IN HEAVEN

I saw that in Heaven, there is a standard of excellence that is beyond comprehension. Because there are no needs in Heaven, every person experiences extreme joy and contentment. Wealth is abundant in the heavenly Kingdom and this is God's character—He likes expensive things. In the beginning, God made this earth perfect, and He is now building His spiritual Kingdom on the earth. If we are to join with Him in the covenant, we must realize that God has placed in each of us a unique sphere of influence. He's given us gifts, talents, and abilities so that we can present and implement Heaven's solutions and strategies into the earth. Christians everywhere can join in what God is doing. You will encounter the realm of Heaven's abundance and blessing as you work with His Kingdom to bring in the end-time harvest!

Supernatural finance is the invisible realm of God's Kingdom that has a financial system that will help every Christian to accomplish Kingdom strategies. It is time to know God's will for your life. The Holy Spirit can give you discernment to know and understand His will. There are specific battle strategies against the enemies of God that are coming to those who seek Him. The Holy Spirit wants to share secrets with you on how to become debt-free and walk in divine favor in this life.

Remember that you have a supernatural advantage when you allow the Holy Spirit to give you access to the unlimited supply of

Heaven's economic system. Your journey with Him will take you into the understanding of how to engage and partner with the Holy Spirit in your finances. The ultimate goal of the Holy Spirit is for you to step right into the most significant move of God the world has ever seen!

ASK AND RECEIVE

We will receive in prayer *everything we ask* when God dwells with us. The act of handing over everything during visitation and allowing Him to move in and live with you will produce the highest efficiency in prayer. The Holy Spirit will honor the covenant you have with God and will not let you ask amiss. God will positively respond to your requests as you visit with Him. He loves you, and you love Him. Answered prayer makes your joy full (see John 15:11). Because you abide in Him and He abides in you, He gives you *whatever you desire.*

> *If you abide in Me, and My words abide in you, you will ask what **you desire**, and it shall be done for you. By this My Father is glorified, that you bear much fruit; so you will be My disciples* (John 15:7-8).

Turn to Him in the darkest hour—God is preparing you entirely so that the supernatural can occur in your life.

Have you ever noticed how hard it is to pray in the *dark hours* of your life? You may experience grief in situations you are facing and do not always feel like turning to God because of those feelings. However, when you are hurting and in trouble, that is the very time that you need to turn to Him. "Therefore humble yourselves under the mighty hand of God, that He may exalt you in due time, casting all your care upon Him, for He cares for you" (1 Peter 5:6-7). The most important thing to remember about the heavenly realm is that you must yield to that realm. When you yield to the heavenly realm, the Comforter will visit you. Prayer will become a breath of Heaven as you effectively pray by the Spirit. "But the Comforter (Counselor, Helper, Intercessor, Advocate, Strengthener, Standby), the Holy Spirit, Whom the Father will send in My name [in My place, to represent Me and act on My behalf], He will teach you all things" (John 14:26 AMPC).

The word *Comforter* (Strong's number G3875) is the Greek word *parakletos* (par-ak-lay-tos), which means an intercessor, consoler. Did you notice the six words that the Amplified Bible uses to describe the word Comforter? Counselor, Helper, Intercessor, Advocate, Strengthener, Standby.

I remember a time when the Holy Spirit clearly became my counselor concerning my retirement. I was praying in the Spirit for a couple of hours one day about a strategy for investing my money in a retirement fund. I wanted to invest wisely so that when we did retire, we would have enough finances to live on the rest of lives. All of a sudden, I had a breakthrough inside and burst forth with joy. I saw clearly before my eyes the exact amount that I would have in my retirement fund when I retired years later. I had such a victory note in my spirit when I saw the future that I stopped praying. I knew that I had broken through with the answer at that moment. I got my answer that day, but I did not retire for sixteen more years. On the day I retired I transferred all my funds for retirement out into another account. When it was all said and done the amount that I had in the account was exactly what I saw in the Spirit sixteen years prior. The Holy Spirit was counseling me on my future and telling me not to be concerned. The Spirit is speaking that to you now. As you seek the Lord with all your heart, He is going to give you desires of your heart. Your heavenly Father has your future written in advance in Heaven (see Ps. 139:16).

SATAN FIGHTS TRUTH

Satan fights the truth about speaking in tongues almost as much as any other subject. He opposes this because it is of vital importance that every believer in these last days be filled with the Spirit and speak in other tongues as the Spirit gives utterance. Speaking in tongues exists so that the truth may be known and proclaimed through your mouth. In the Book of James, he teaches that the tongue is the member of the body that controls the whole body. So, if the Spirit of God can get hold of a believer's tongue, then the Spirit of God can get hold of your life. This is the reason why the Holy Spirit takes hold of your tongue when you are baptized with the Holy Spirit. Additionally, Romans 12:2-3 reveals that the soul is not saved through the born-again experience, but it must be transformed by the renewing of your mind by the Word of God. Our mind, emotions, and will, those three parts of our soul, must be renewed daily and be sanctified through our obedience to the Word.

The apostle James talks about the tongue being set on fire by the flames of hell and how through the Holy Spirit a person's tongue can be set on fire by the Holy Spirit. When our tongue is set on fire by the Holy Spirit, we are speaking the truth in love and ful-filling the purpose for which the church was formed. Our bodies together as the Christian church represent Christ's Body. The Holy Spirit is here to unify the Body of Christ, the church, until we come into the fullness of Him who bought us. See the books of Ephesians and Colossians for clarification of these principles.

Therefore, anyone can understand how important it is to allow ourselves to operate in the spirit world by yielding the members of our body to the Spirit. We yield our members by speaking in other tongues. We also must walk in the Spirit by submitting our flesh to the Spirit of God. By yielding to speak in tongues and by walking in the Spirit, we can begin to operate in the unseen realm where angels complete their missions. When we yield our mouths to speaking in tongues and our spirits to walking in the Word, we begin to live according to God's Word daily. As you speak the truth in a prayer that has been sent from Heaven, which contains a perfect prayer, your spirit speaks forth the truth. When your spirit speaks forth truth, the angels gather around you because they recognize that you have connected fully with their mission. Their mission is to see to it that you have what you need to walk out the plan and purpose of God for your life on this earth, and that includes your *supernatural finances*.

PRAY IN TONGUES

Sometimes we do not have the ability to pray effectively because of our limitations. I always encourage people to know what their weaknesses are and yield to the "Greater One" within them. If you do not know how you should pray in any situation, yield to the Holy Spirit and the baptism of the Holy Spirit. "Likewise the Spirit also helps in our weaknesses. For we do not know what we should pray for as we ought, but the Spirit Himself makes intercession for us with groanings which cannot be uttered" (Rom. 8:26)—to help you pray in any situation. He will give you words to speak that are not in your language. However, those words are going directly to God and automatically asking for the correct thing.

> Jesus taught me in my heavenly visitation that the single most important thing I could do to participate in the supernatural realm was to pray in tongues.

When you yield to the Holy Spirit in this way and speak in other tongues, you cannot utter a wrong prayer. Praying in tongues is the perfect prayer. It is free, and it has already been given. All you need to do is to take care and not lean on your understanding and yield to the greater One within you. He knows how to pray for you and get the job done. Our enemy fights this more than anything because he knows he cannot win against people who will allow the Holy Spirit to pray through them. That should tell you something about yielding and letting the Holy One pray through you. The apostle Paul said:

> *When someone speaks in tongues, no one understands a word he says, because he's not speaking to people, but to God—he is speaking intimate mysteries in the Spirit. But when someone prophesies, he speaks to encourage people, to build them up, and to bring them comfort.*

> *The one who speaks in tongues advances his own spiritual progress, while the one who prophesies builds up the church* (1 Corinthians 14:2-4 TPT).

So go ahead and speak by the power of God and let your destiny and purpose be prayed out and spoken into existence as you enjoy the *supernatural finances* that God has prepared for you!

Chapter 2

Praying in the Spirit and Supernatural Provision

I thank God that I speak in tongues more than any of you (1 Corinthians 14:18 NLT).

When I had the experience of being with Jesus for forty-five minutes in 1992, Jesus spoke to me concerning praying in the Spirit. It was one of the most important subjects that Jesus discussed. Praying in the Spirit involves using our spirit to yield our tongue to the utterance of the Holy Spirit. God will allow us to speak mysteries from the depths of God's heart through the depths our spirit. This activity is for our personal fellowship with God. When we are in a public assembly, the gift of prophecy is more effective in building everyone up than speaking in tongues unless someone has the gift of interpretation. People must be able to understand what is actually said or it is of no value to others. The apostle Paul said:

> *For if you have the ability to speak in tongues, you will be talking only to God, since people won't be able to understand you. You will be speaking by the power of the Spirit, but it will all be mysterious. But one who prophesies strengthens others, encourages them, and comforts them. **A person who speaks in tongues is strengthened personally, but one who speaks a word of prophecy strengthens the entire church.** I wish you could all speak in tongues, but even more I wish you could all prophesy. For prophecy is greater than speaking in tongues, unless someone interprets what you are saying so that the whole church will be strengthened* (1 Corinthians 14:2-5 NLT).

Jesus taught me that this was the single most important activity you could engage in that would open the door to the supernatural. Because of this statement, I have a sense of obligation to discuss it often in my teaching sessions. We can have both the ability to speak in tongues and to interpret them as the Spirit wills. Yielding to the gift of prophecy and speaking the mysteries of God can be performed in our own known language.

SPIRITUAL ACTIVITY

Remember that this activity is the way to engage the Holy Spirit in such a way that we can utter perfect prayers to the heavenly Father. Paul told the Corinthians:

That is what the Scriptures mean when they say, "No eye has seen, no ear has heard, and no mind has imagined what God has prepared for those who love him." But it was to us that God revealed these things by his Spirit. For his Spirit searches out everything and shows us God's deep secrets. No one can know a person's thoughts except that person's own spirit, and no one can know God's thoughts except God's own Spirit. And we have received God's Spirit (not the world's spirit), so we can know the wonderful things God has freely given us. When we tell you these things, we do not use words that come from human wisdom. Instead, we speak words given to us by the Spirit, using the Spirit's words to explain spiritual truths. But people who aren't spiritual can't receive these truths from God's Spirit. It all sounds foolish to them and they can't understand it, for only those who are spiritual can understand what the Spirit means (1 Corinthians 2:9-14 NLT).

In First Corinthians 14:18, Paul made this statement about tongues: "I thank my God I speak with tongues more than you all." The apostle Paul was a supporter of speaking in tongues and spoke in tongues more than anyone else in the church. He was talking to the church at Corinth, and they spoke in tongues a great deal. Paul had to talk to them about the misuse of many of the nine spiritual gifts. There is a process of learning how to operate in the Spirit concerning praying in tongues. Praying in tongues is tied to our personal walk with God and includes all aspects of our lives. Praying in tongues is also tied to our personal walk with God, and that includes even the financial realm as well.

> The Spirit of God desires to lead us into all truth. The enemy desires to lead us into deception—this includes our finances.

The Spirit of God reveals the truth about our finances and God's Kingdom. The earthly physical realm that is visible, here in this world, is ruled by satan. Most people are unaware that he controls the financial world of this planet. It does not matter to him that most people on earth have no understanding that he has control of the financial world. As we know by experience, the enemy's control is an evil weapon. Satan also uses fear to control people. If we look at the financial system, it has fear and control built into it. So, the Holy Spirit wants us to know the truth and be set free. The Lord wanted me to come back and tell people the truth about what I saw and heard. People need to know Jesus' intent for their life. One of the things that He has told me to talk about is supernatural finances because people are afraid to let God into their finances. If they did understand God's intent for them personally concerning finances, they would open the door wide for the Lord to instruct them and guide them in their financial situations.

REVELATION AND THE TONGUE

Eventually, through a revelation of the Spirit, people will begin to see that we have financial freedom and that God provides a way to set us free. Our heavenly Father desires to help us and prosper us in everything we do. During the heavenly vision I had with Jesus in 1992, Jesus gave me the mandate to help His people under-stand and begin to move in supernatural financial freedom. I was in an operation that involved oral surgery. During the time period of my surgery, the Lord spent time talking with me. He revealed many of the truths that I speak concerning the other realm called the "Realm of the Spirit." I was privileged to see the other realm. I actually was participating in the heavenly realm. One of the reasons that Jesus took me into the heavenly realm was to give me valuable information to share with believers so that they could comprehend supernatural finances, and also so that I could explain the way that they could move into supernatural financial blessings.

During the visitation in 1992, the Lord taught me how to yield to the Holy Spirit and how to pray in the Spirit. Jesus revealed to me how important yielding to the Spirit and praying in the Spirit are to obtaining victory in life. He emphasized information about praying in the Spirit concerning spiritual authority.

My first book, called *Heavenly Visitation,* contains a step-by-step account of the very biblical teachings that Jesus covered when I had that visitation with Him. A Christian will have to learn to yield to the Spirit to begin to have revelation concerning the myster-ies of God. Speaking in other tongues is an activity that will reveal the mysteries that God knows His children need to have victory in every area of their lives. In First Corinthians 2, Paul said that we need to pray in tongues. He stressed that the Spirit searches the deep things of God. He told of how the mysteries remain hidden, except when the Spirit reveals them. We do have the revelation of the Spirit of God within each one of us, but we must to yield to Him to gain that revelation knowledge.

One way that we can yield to Him is by allowing the Holy Spirit to take over our tongue. When the Holy Spirit prays out the mysteries of God through us, it is in another language. When speaking in tongues happens, the Holy Spirit is actually praying out those mysteries through our voices in our spiritual language. We just yield ourselves to the leading of the Lord and open our mouths to speak forth in a language that we never knew before that time, and perhaps it may be even in a language that we do not understand as we speak it forth. This experience is referred to as the baptism of the Holy Spirit. If a person does not have that experience, I believe that they should ask God to baptize them in His Spirit. (To understand this, concentrate on the book of First Corinthians, especially chapters 12, 13, and 14. Also, study First Corinthians 2.)

OBSERVATIONS

Jesus taught me that the single most important activity that we can do to participate in the supernatural is to speak in tongues. Jesus Himself said that He gave the Spirit on the day of Pentecost when the outpouring of the Holy Spirit happened in Jerusalem. Many different people observed what happened on that day. The number-one observation that is important to notice is that God was able to cause what happened on that day because they were all in one accord. The people, about one hundred twenty of them in the upper room, were in unity. The second observation is that when the Holy Spirit came on the day of Pentecost there was a mighty rushing wind. The third observation is that with that wind there came tongues of fire resting on their heads.

The fourth observation is that they started to speak in other languages that they did not even know themselves. The believers spoke in tongues. It is recorded that the people encountered utterance in a supernatural language. The fifth and final observation is that they also appeared to be drunk on alcohol. This was not the case. It was the middle of the day, and Peter got up and said, "These are not drunk, as you suppose" (Acts 2:15). Peter then referred back to the prophet Joel. The prophet Joel prophesied that this event would happen. These are the events that occurred when the Holy Spirit came.

Jesus taught us that we should yield to the Holy Spirit because He is our Helper. In Romans 8:26, we see that the apostle Paul said, "We don't even know how to pray" and are weak (TPT). He said that in our weakness, the Holy Spirit is going to come in, take hold of us, and make us strong. We are going to start to pray supernatural prayers. We are going to be able to pray out the will God.

When we begin to verbalize our prayer, it is not going to be in our own known language. It is going to be in a language that is led by the Holy Spirit. The idea is that as we yield to the Spirit and get strengthened, we start to pray out the mysteries of God. The truth comes by revelation supernaturally. Jesus said that when we allow the Spirit to lead, He will lead us into everything that is true. When we discuss the financial realm, a believer can see that poverty is not what God has for His people. That mystery will become obvious to those who are able to pray things out in tongues. Poverty is because of the curse, according to Deuteronomy 28.

Blessings and Curses

Deuteronomy 28 says that God is blessing people who are obedient to Him and who follow Him. If He is blessing them and causing them to prosper, it is the direct opposite of what the curse causes. In Deuteronomy 28, God reveals information about the curses that can come upon man. These curses list all the bad things that are going to happen if a person does not adhere to what the Lord has commanded. If a person does not do what is commanded, he is going to be cursed. Jesus told me that the Holy Spirit wants to be a Helper who will pull alongside us and actually to bring us into the truth. All the blessings that are available to us are found in Deuteronomy 28.

We have got to allow the Holy Spirit to take over our tongue and pray "in the Spirit." When we do allow the Holy Spirit to take over, then we are inviting God to engage in our lives in the supernatural realm. This includes opening our financial situations up to Him so that He can bless us tremendously with not only great wealth but understanding of how to obtain and maintain great wealth. We are praying out the mysteries as we have just read. We are not praying to a man; we are praying to God. God is hearing everything we are saying. If we have not come to the stage of interpreting our spiritual language into something we know, and we do not understand what we are saying, God does understand what we are saying. We yield to the gift of the Spirit by praying in tongues, the heavenly gift. We also can interpret what we are saying. There is an interpretation at times that can come forth. Alternatively, we could yield to the gift of prophecy, which means we speak in our own language and do not need an interpretation, but what we speak is actually speaking forth the mysteries of God in our known language. Tongues and interpretation can work together to reveal meaning of what God has prayed through our yielding to Him. Prophecy, on the other hand, needs no interpretation as a step. It is spoken in the language that we know.

A person can do all of these things in prayer by yielding to the Spirit and allowing the Spirit to speak prophetically through them. Out of a believer's mouth come proclamations concerning the mysteries of God. Start to yield to the Spirit, and He is going to lead us into all truth. He is going to lead us into the blessings that are the truthful way, the proper way to go. Truth always prevails and is the way to prosper. Truth says we are the head, not the tail. Truth says we are to be above, not beneath so we will have things to lend, but we will not have to borrow. The same Holy Spirit of the Old Testament is the Holy Spirit of the New Testament.

It is time to be prepared for a great move of God. The Holy Spirit is going to lead us into the blessings of Deuteronomy 28. There is no difference between the God of the Old Testament and the New Testament. What we have available to us now is the result of the revelation that has increased through Jesus Christ. That revelation has brought us into the fullness and the fulfillment of what Jesus did. So what is the Holy Spirit saying now? It is time to find out what truth He may be leading us toward in our lives. If a person lacks understanding, they may not be ready to fully accept great things that are possible at that time because they have false information. The Holy Spirit reveals truth to God's own so that they might have great victory in all things and be overcomers.

As believers, we need to ask ourselves, "Are we going to believe a lie or are we going to believe the truth?" It is a terrible thing for a believer to know that a person has been deceived but still chooses to stay in deception. I am not comfortable leaving a meeting or a conference knowing that people are still not fully understanding the blessings that God has for them because they are willing to remain deceived. I do not like that. I want everyone to be able to participate in the promised blessing that I saw belong to God's family. Those blessings are the ones that I saw in the heavenly realms when I met with the Lord Jesus in 1992. I would love to be able to take people's hands and take them with me to the same place that Jesus took me. Then, they would be able to see and understand the same insight that I received from my meeting with Jesus. Unfortunately, I cannot take them there to show them what I learned in that place. However, I can share the things that I learned when Jesus met with me, and those things will help others to have not only financial victory but victory in all areas of life if they will hear truth and apply what they have learned.

We teach the truth and let the Spirit reveal. He is a revealer of truth, as First Corinthians 2:9-14 says:

> *"No eye has seen, no ear has heard, and no mind has imagined what God has prepared for those who love him." But it was to us that God revealed these things by his Spirit. For his Spirit searches out everything and shows us God's deep secrets. No one can know a person's thoughts except that person's own spirit, and no one can know God's thoughts except God's own Spirit. And we have received God's Spirit (not the world's spirit), so we can know the wonderful things God has freely given us. When we tell you these things, we do not use words that come from human wisdom. Instead, we speak words given to us by the Spirit, using the Spirit's words to explain spiritual truths. But people who aren't spiritual can't receive these truths from God's Spirit. It all sounds foolish to them and they can't understand it, for only those who are spiritual can understand what the Spirit means* (NLT).

EYES THAT SEE

Whatever it is you are going through right now, whatever it is that you need in this physical realm, you have to understand that God already knows what that is. His Spirit has come so that we can enjoy these things in this life right now in the physical realm. What is it that is lacking? Is there a need? The Holy Spirit is saying to us right now there is a supernatural provision available. There are all kinds of essential plans unfolding right now all around us. I can sense it by the Spirit. Something is going on with the Body of Christ right now in Jesus's name!

When I was in heaven, I saw that God's Spirit was with us to help us to see what we could not see in the spirit realm.

If we could see what is going on around us that is not visible with physical eyes, there would be excitement in our hearts. The Spirit of God is desiring to reveal that to us. Those things that are hidden from us right now concerning our finances are supernaturally coming into full understanding. So when we pray by the Spirit, we are praying out the truth of God; we are overcoming the physical as we accelerate into the spiritual.

As we mature, our eyes are enlightened. A person who is in the process of maturing will start to see things that they could not see before. These things are the truth or reality. What is it right now that is bothering you? The Spirit wants to tell us truths concerning our finances so that we do not have to be in the dark anymore. I am saying this by the Spirit of God. I understand that we need to hear this truth. We need to take ourselves into the prayer closet and shut ourselves off from all the influence of the world. Christians need to allow God Himself to talk to them and show us how to obtain the rest of God in His Kingdom. We can do that if we pray in tongues and *allow the Spirit of God to dictate what to think and what to say and hear.* Let the Holy Spirit create an environment of Heaven around us.

Here is an important key: Let the Spirit create the environment of Heaven around you. When I came back to this realm, I saw that I had to create an environment of Heaven around myself. It was a spiritual battle that I had to fight for years because the devil did not want me to enter into the place where I could have the environment of Heaven around me. Satan was hopeful that I would let the revelation that I had received just fade away. Just because I had God reveal all of these wonderful things to me did not mean these victories were going to start to come to pass in my life. I was in Heaven, and I experienced being there, but I still had to live my life out down here. And to be honest, living these things out in life here has not been easy. I have had to fight many spiritual battles to have the victories finally come to pass.

I did learn from the things that I suffered, as well as from implementing the things that I knew needed to be done. I am teaching you. I can save you much time and hurt if you will listen to me. Here is another key. We will have to pray out of our weakness. We cannot pray out of our strength. In other words, it is all right to feel weak and to feel as if we cannot pray. Sometimes we cannot see or hear what is going on in the spirit realm. However, in our weakness, not in our strength, the Spirit of God will come, and He will be present to help us pray.

He is a Stand-by, the One who is ready to act as we pray:

1. He is going to be an advocate for us.

2. He is going to be an enforcer for us.

3. He is going to be the One who breaks the power of the curse for us.

4. He is willing to bring us into the new-covenant benefits.

As a believer in Jesus Christ, the Spirit God has come to be with us; however, we must participate in this supernatural event every day. It is called praying in the Spirit.

PRAYING OUT OF WEAKNESS

I want you to know that when you pray in the Spirit out of your own inability to comprehend and perform, you are in a good position for the Holy Spirit to step in and accomplish God's will on your behalf.

We do not always know the best way to pray. When you are going through a trial, you need understanding so that you can stand firm in your faith. God has given us help through the wonderful Holy Spirit. He will help you when you feel weak. He only wants the Father God's best for you.

The apostle Paul said this:

> *And the Holy Spirit helps us in our weakness. For example, we don't know what God wants us to pray for. But the Holy Spirit prays for us with groanings that cannot be expressed in words. And the Father who knows all hearts knows what the Spirit is saying, **for the Spirit pleads for us believers in harmony with God's own will**. And we know that God causes everything to work together for the good of those who love God and are called according to his purpose for them* (Romans 8:26-28 NLT).

I have found that when I yield to the Spirit of God in my weakness, He prays out the mysteries of God. The result is that the will of God is done and everything always works out for my good. God has honestly given us a powerful advocate to help us to pray more effectively.

Romans 8:26-28 is an exciting scripture, which we should always have available every time we pray. The Holy Spirit has been sent to help us to express our heart to God in words that we cannot articulate on our own. Jesus told me that if we will yield to this process of praying in the Spirit, we are participating in the supernatural. The more we do pray in the Spirit during our day, the more the Spirit of God will have preeminence in our lives.

He will lead us into all truth, which will then lead us into financial freedom and prosperity. The Lord wants us to prosper. It is His will for us. He does not, however, want us to be controlled by a desire for wealth.

So I have found that if I yield to the Spirit of God in weakness, I become strong almost immediately. I have, over the years, realized that when I feel weak, it is a divine setup. I know that there is a move of God about to happen in my life. So remember to pray out the mysteries as the Holy Spirit guides you in praying in tongues. The result is the will of God will be done and everything will to work out fine. That is what I know.

By His Spirit, God is continually speaking freedom into the lives of His people. When they pray in their heavenly language, He is speaking through them and talking about a breakthrough in their lives. God is announcing victory over His people continually. The Holy Spirit is announcing the future for believers everywhere. When we speak in tongues, the Holy Spirit is breaking the curse in our lives and enforcing the blessing in our lives. This is exciting because the Holy Spirit desires to walk into our future with us, and it will be a good future. So if God is going to bring you into your destiny—the Spirit of Truth is going to walk you into it. The Holy Spirit does not know anything else but the fulfillment of what the Lord has said is to come.

In this hour of revelation of the church, we are seated with Him in the heavenly realms. One of the truths that must come to the forefront is this—we must yield to the move of the Spirit of God.

THE SPIRIT OF TRUTH

*But the hour is coming, and now is, when the true worshipers will worship the Father in **spirit and truth**;*

*for the Father is seeking such to worship Him. God is Spirit, and those who worship Him must worship in **spirit and truth*** (John 4:23-24).

Another aspect of *absolute truth* in the earth is this: the Holy Spirit was sent to us. Through this mighty member of the Trinity, we can experience the power, presence, and authority of God Himself. One of the most important things to know about the Holy Spirit is that He is the Spirit of truth. Jesus announced that the Holy Spirit was coming:

> *If you love Me, keep My commandments. And I will pray the Father, and He will give you another Helper, that He may abide with you forever—**the Spirit of truth**, whom the world cannot receive, because it neither sees Him nor knows Him; but you know Him, for He dwells with you and will be in you. I will not leave you orphans; I will come to you* (John 14:15-18).

The Holy Spirit dwells inside of us to speak and testify of God. When we pray in the Spirit, we pray out the mysteries of God. Without the Holy Spirit guiding our prayers in the Spirit, we would not know how to pray correctly. The Holy Spirit helps us to pray a perfect prayer that coordinates entirely with God's Word and with His will for our lives. The angels gather together around us as we pray out the mysteries. They are not mysteries to the angels because they hear the will of the Lord as we speak forth, and they are ready to act. Remember that when we pray in the Spirit, we, in reality, yield to the throne room of God and His authority.

> *And in a similar way, the Holy Spirit takes hold of us in our human frailty to empower us in our weakness.*

For example, at times we don't even know how to pray, or know the best things to ask for. But the Holy Spirit rises up within us to super-intercede on our behalf, pleading to God with emotional sighs too deep for words (Romans 8:26 TPT).

> When we testify by the Spirit about Jesus, we are yielding to the Spirit of prophecy (see Rev. 19:10). We are allowing the Holy Spirit to speak absolute truth from the Throne.

*But when the Helper comes, whom I shall send to you from the Father, the Spirit of truth who proceeds from the Father, He will **testify of Me**. And you also will bear witness, because you have been with Me from the beginning* (John 15:26-27).

It Has Begun

The most significant move of the Spirit that ever will happen in the history of the world has begun. It is time for every Christian to let go of his life and give that life entirely to God. Each Christian must make Jesus Lord over his entire life today.

It is time to have any chains of bondage broken in every Christian's life. As every Christian yields to God, he releases anything that has been an anchor that keeps him from completely serving God. When all of those hindrances are gone, great things can begin to happen. Jesus had many things to say to us, and He told us that He would send the Holy Spirit to lead us into all truth. He said:

> *I still have many things to say to you, but you cannot bear them now. However, when He, **the Spirit of truth, has come, He will guide you into all truth**; for He will not speak on His own authority, but whatever He hears He will speak; and He will tell you things to come. He will glorify Me, for He will take of what is Mine and declare it to you. All things that the Father has are Mine. Therefore I said that He will take of Mine and declare it to you* (John 16:12-15).

There is an absolute truth of God in Heaven. The Holy Spirit will take that message of truth and give it to you. He can make His truth your environment so you can encounter the victorious atmosphere of Heaven on the earth. And this is because the Holy Spirit has been given to us. He will create an atmosphere of Heaven. Jesus announced that the Holy Spirit was coming and said:

> *If you love Me, keep My commandments. And I will pray the Father, and He will give you another Helper, that He may abide with you forever—the Spirit of truth, whom the world cannot receive, because it neither sees Him nor knows Him; but you know Him, for He dwells with you and will be in you. I will not leave you orphans; I will come to you* (John 14:15-18).

We have the promise that the Holy Spirit is not only coming to us but will never leave us. We have an encouraging word from Jesus. Think about how hard it is to be down here with the warfare that happens. The fact is that the world system is in place; we cannot win against it, especially concerning debt in our finances. Everything is in place to put us into debt or to keep us in debt for the rest of our lives and without any possibility to have an inheritance to give to our children. The will of God is for us to be able to give to our children's children an abundant inheritance.

Giving to the Gospel is also an important part of God's plan for a believer's life. Supernatural finances will come to you because the Gospel message is free, but the way to get financial blessings to people is not free. There are all kinds of bills people must pay because people just do not give you free things. Often, people expect a minister to give what they have to give to people for no cost to them. They do not understand the fact that everyone must be paid for the work he does. Ministers must eat and pay bills. God wants us all to prosper.

The Lord wants all of us to have more than enough to support what He is doing through His people in the earth. Then, the message can be free for those who will receive it. But the way to get the message to people is not that it takes people. It takes finances to pay the bills. God is saying that it is important to listen to His direction when He says, "If you love Me, keep My commandments." The Lord promised that He would pray, and He would give us another Comforter. And this is the Spirit of Truth. The Spirit of Truth is going to dwell in you and be with you. He will never leave you, and no matter what you feel like right at this very moment, remember that you are never alone.

The Holy Spirit wants to lead you into things that pertain to your future. The things in your future do relate to supernatural finances because you work for a living. You have bills to pay. You need wealth to come to you so that you can take care of all your commitments and then have extra to give to others. You are supposed to help others and support the work of God. Your support should be given into whatever place the Lord directs you to give. Supernatural finances definitely have to do with the Holy Spirit. Supernatural finances are part of God's plan for you on earth.

God is not only concerned about your mental health, about your physical health, about your relationships, about where you go to church, and about your future. He is also concerned about your finances. He wants to be in the battle to win victory in your finances with you. The Holy Spirit who is inside of us already knows exactly what our condition happens to be. He wants you to know how to tap into the Holy Spirit within you. Information from God's throne is being sent into your spirit. When you speak in tongues, you speak the answers to the needs you face. Praying in tongues will help you to win the battles you face. The way to victory is already within you. He wants you to understand that there are ways to walk out of whatever problem you are facing. If you are in debt and you need help, God can begin to give you words and tell you how to solve those problems step by step.

That is what He did for my wife and me. We did the things that He spoke through us to do. We went step by step, and we found ourselves out of debt and prospering. However, it did take a process of time. It actually took about seven years. We worked really hard, we gave, and we did everything that God's Word said to do. We helped other people, and we rejoice. It was fun for us to give because we were giving to God. We were not giving to men. We were not doing anything for man's approval. We are doing it for God, and God saw our hearts and rewarded us. He will do the same for you as well.

The Holy Spirit will help you to pray out perfect prayers and to walk out of doing things in the flesh. Everything that He has planned for you that causes increase and not decrease will be in the blessing and not in the curse. You will be a lender and not a borrower. You will move out of the world system by getting out of debt. You will lend, and you will not borrow anymore. *When you pray in the Spirit, you are actually yielding to the throne room of God.* The Holy Spirit is only going to do the will of God, and you will therefore be set free financially.

ALLOWING THE HOLY SPIRIT TO MOVE UPON YOU IN PRAYER

Have you ever imagined what it was like when the "mighty rushing wind" came on the Day of Pentecost? I have, and I know that the same type of great move of God is starting again because Heaven is visiting us in these last days. The Holy Spirit is the Master of the spirit realm. The supernatural is the Holy Spirit's everyday environment. The breath of God and the Holy Spirit are one. Jesus even breathed on His disciples one day and said, "Receive the Holy Spirit."

As we learn about the mighty Holy Spirit, remember that He is to be treated as part of the Godhead. He is part of the Godhead and is expressed through wind, breath, fire, gifts, a dove, a liberator, an attorney, power, and authority—just to name a few. But remember, He is a Person and part of the Holy Trinity. He can be grieved. He is known in the Kingdom for righteousness, peace, and joy. Paul said, "For the kingdom of God is not eating and drinking, but righteousness and peace and joy in the Holy Spirit. For he who serves Christ in these things is acceptable to God and approved by men" (Rom. 14:17-18).

When we pray in the Holy Spirit, we are participating in the Kingdom of God. The one who prays and is accepted by God serves in these three things—righteousness, peace, and joy in the Holy Spirit. When Jesus taught me to pray, He showed me that I would encounter these three attributes, as well as the *resurrection power* that raised Jesus from the dead (see Eph. 2:5).

THE SPIRIT LIVING IN YOU

When I pray under the influence of the Holy Spirit, I can sense the powers of the coming age spoken of in the book of Hebrews (see Heb. 6:5). This working of power has the ability to influence every part of your being. The mighty power will enable you to pray yourself right into the answer that you need.

As you yield to the mighty Holy Spirit, He is taking you on to greater heights. These heights are places where you can stand within His ability. You are able to see into the future that you could not see before moving into these heights. Your view was obstructed due to your former vantage point. He will unveil your purpose—that purpose which was recorded long ago. Your purpose was written from the Father's heart for you and now is revealed by the Holy Spirit. Yield to the Spirit of the living God and you will pray in a way that moves you into your destiny. Do not delay the entrance into the spirit realm. Pray and yield to that which the Spirit is saying. Now is the time to allow Him to pray out the mysteries of God through you! Ask yourself, "What is the Holy Spirit saying to me about praying out the mysteries?"

The Holy Spirit has the capability of raising people from the dead. He was the One who was involved in that process. Jesus told me when I had my that He had such a relationship with the Father God and the Holy Spirit that He had to trust them when He died and went to hell. For the full account of this story, please see my previous book entitled *Heavenly Visitation*. He said with a broken voice,

"I had to trust that the Father would give the command on the third day for the Holy Spirit to raise Me from the dead." The power of the Holy Spirit broke Him out of the hellish prison and brought Him back to life in His earthly body. He is the Resurrection and the Life. The Holy Spirit was the Person who enabled Christ to rise to life. So when you pray, you must remember that very same power is available and effectual when we pray fervently (see James 5:16).

Now is the time to allow Him to pray out the mysteries of God through you!

Things to Remember

1. We have the life of God in us.

2. He wants to pray through us.

3. He will quicken us.

The Spirit of God, who raised Jesus from the dead, lives in you. And just as God raised Christ Jesus from the dead, he will give life to your mortal bodies by this same Spirit living within you (Romans 8:11 NLT).

4. It is time for the Holy Spirit to get our bodies energized with the life of God.

5. Let faith rise up in our heart and tell our soul to trust in God.

Why are you cast down, O my soul? And why are you disquieted within me? Hope in God, for I shall yet praise Him for the help of His countenance (Psalm 42:5).

BEING FILLED WITH THE SPIRIT

It is very important to be filled with the Spirit of God. Let Him continually flow as rivers of living water out of you as you begin to pray in the Spirit (see John 7:38).

Therefore do not be unwise, but understand what the will of the Lord is. And do not be drunk with wine, in which is dissipation; but be filled with the Spirit, speaking to one another in psalms and hymns and spiritual songs, singing and making melody in your heart to the Lord, giving thanks always for all things to God the Father in the name of our Lord Jesus Christ, submitting to one another in the fear of God (Ephesians 5:17-21).

I remember when we were looking for a house in New Orleans after the Lord had called us to live there. We would come down and stay in a hotel every month for two weeks at a time. We did that for several months and could not find the right house. We prayed in the Holy Spirit for hours each day, and then we would return to Phoenix to work for the remainder of each month. My wife and I were told by the Lord to sow an offering into a ministry toward breakthrough for our house. Within a couple of hours, we found our house. Finally, the answer arrived. The answer came only after continually offering thanksgiving to God, sowing financially into our church, and praying forth the mysteries in the Spirit. On separate occasions, we had two different friends tell us that the Lord had the house and that He was hiding it *for us*, not hiding it *from us*. Then suddenly, our answer came to us supernaturally. We could not do it on our own, and He came through for us.

Six Characteristics of Someone Living a Spirit-filled Life Are:

1. They understand what the Lord's will for their life is.

2. They are not drunk with wine, but are filled with the Spirit.

3. They speak to one another in psalms, hymns, and spiritual songs.

4. They sing and make melody in their heart to the Lord.

5. They give thanks to their Father God.

6. They submit to one another in the fear of God.

If are to break evil spirits, *we can start by talking about Jesus to people we encounter* from our spirit by the Holy Spirit. Testify about how real Jesus is and how much authority He has. Testify of how He has defeated the enemy, satan, and how God has a book written about every individual that is on the shelves in Heaven. Testify about Jesus' faithfulness, and tell them that they need to accept Jesus as their Lord and Savior.

Let people know that they will be adopted into the family of God through the blood of Jesus. Tell the people that when they confess their sins to God, their sins have been washed away by the blood of Jesus. He is no longer angry with them if they will accept this Gospel message. As we yield to the Spirit and the Spirit of prophecy comes forth, we start to testify about Jesus. Testifying about Jesus is the Spirit of prophecy. John 15:26 says that when the Helper comes, the Spirit will testify of Jesus, and we will also bear witness. The Holy Spirit will begin to testify through us and cause you us to have favor with man and with God. Then you will be ready to actively participate in the greatest move of the Spirit that has ever happened. And that move of God is, at this time, right before us!

Chapter 3

Accessing Battle Strategies Concerning Giving and Receiving: Part One

There was a famine in the land. ...Then Isaac sowed in that land [in spite of famine], and reaped in the same year a hundredfold; and the Lord blessed him. The man began to prosper, and continued prospering until he became very prosperous (Genesis 26:1,12-13).

THE LORD GOD HAS A SUPERNATURAL BATTLE STRATEGY concerning your giving and receiving in the Kingdom of God. We live in a system that is taken over by the spirit of this world. Satan desires to keep everyone under his control by either giving them great wealth at the sacrifice of their eternal life with Jesus or by imprisoning people in excessive debt so that they are never free. The fact is, God is willing for all to prosper and be in good health!

> *Beloved, I pray that in every way you may suc-*
> *ceed and prosper and be in good health [physically],*
> *just as [I know] your soul prospers [spiritually]*
> (3 John 1:2 AMP).

The next thing I want to discuss is the secret battle strategy concerning supernatural finances. This is very important for your lifestyle—the way you live in this earthly realm. You have to get in contact with the spirit realm through your spirit and then you have to live out your supernatural life in the flesh. Every day the Lord wants you to walk in prosperity. However, there are specific battle strategies that you must be aware of to encounter supernatural finances effectively.

God's Secret Battle Strategy Checklist for Supernatural Finances

The Gift of Giving

The first battle strategy I want to discuss is found in the book of Romans. It says:

> *If you have the grace-gift of encouragement, then use it*
> *often to encourage others.* **If you have the grace-gift**
> **of giving to meet the needs of others, then may you**
> **prosper in your generosity without any fanfare.**
> *If you have the gift of leadership, be passionate about*
> *your leadership. And if you have the gift of showing*
> *compassion, then flourish in your cheerful display of*
> *compassion* (Romans 12:8 TPT).

The Lord wants to distribute wealth among His people. Certain individuals are called to spread that wealth so God will prosper them to fulfill this. It is His plan before these people are born that they are designated to spread wealth for the Kingdom. The angels know this, and they minister for those people and help them to prosper. We are all called to prosper individually in everything that we endeavor to do because it is God's will and He wants us to succeed. However, there are those whom God has designated to be financiers of the Kingdom of God. They will bring in great wealth for the work of God. The prophet Jeremiah says:

> *"For I know the plans I have for you," declares the Lord,*
> *"plans to prosper you and not to harm you, plans to give*
> *you hope and a future"* (Jeremiah 29:11 NIV).

You can see that God has an intention for us to prosper and not to harm us. He plans for us to have a good future. Every believer can rely on and trust in the Lord to do this. And there is no one limiting you in Heaven! God is with you in a mighty way, and He doesn't want you to be hindered in any way financially.

The Lord Will Provide

God wants us to prosper. In the book of Genesis, Abraham called the place "The Lord will provide." Which in Hebrew is Jehovah Jireh. Here is another battle strategy—the Lord will provide. "And Abraham called the name of the place, The-Lord-Will-Provide" (Hebrew: Jehovah-Jireh; Gen. 22:14).

We have to understand that because God Almighty sees everything, He always provides. Your loving heavenly Father knows everything that you are ever going to need, and He has already made plans for that provision to come to you.

When God sees you, He wants to provide for you because you are His child. The Lord has the ability to fix anything for anyone who calls on Him. If Almighty God does not have that item that His child is asking, then He will create it for them! The Lord is powerful and loving.

The Power to Get Wealth

The power of God is supernatural. That power resurrected Jesus. He heals by that same power. Jesus gave His name to us, and His mighty name drives out demons.

In Deuteronomy 8:18 God told Moses "And you shall remember the Lord your God, for it is He who gives you power to get wealth, that He may establish His covenant which He swore to your fathers, as it is this day."

Let me share a battle strategy that we need to remember: God has given us the power and the authority to get wealth. God does this so that He can establish His amazing covenant with us. He made this promise to our forefathers a long time ago and that same promise continues to this day. Remember that God is also confirming His contract with you by giving you authority and power to obtain wealth.

God is moving by His Spirit all the time. Right now, He has come upon you by His Spirit and wants you to prosper in everything that you do. The supernatural finances that happen to you are because you trust in the Lord with all your heart. He leads—then establishes your path. The Spirit leads us into all truth, and one of these truths is the fact that God, your heavenly Father, wants to provide for you as it says in Deuteronomy 28. He wants you to receive the authority and the power He has offered through the name of Jesus. God wants you to confirm the covenant in this realm that He accomplished through Jesus Christ. We have the same promise that God initiated with Abraham but now is complete through Jesus.

Through Jesus Christ, that covenant is for every person. Those who believe in Jesus Christ receive an adoption certificate into the family of God. We are in a contract with Almighty God. Another way that God establishes His covenant is that He gives His people wealth so that they can obtain dominion in this earth realm. It is supernatural, but it's part of the Kingdom of God. The Holy Spirit wants to speak these things to the people of God, but occasionally they will not hear it. It is time to open yourself up to the Spirit of God and allow Him to rearrange things and to change the way that you think so that you can obtain this dominion in the financial realm.

The Lord God is the supreme authority of all creation. If a person makes a covenant, he or she should choose someone who is of higher power and greater provision than themselves. Through the new covenant, God desires for every single one of His children to participate fully in the promises. The covenant started with Abraham and now is complete through Jesus Christ for everyone. One of the ways that God establishes His covenant is by giving His people the power to get wealth according to the word given to Moses.

You Shall Reign

Our mighty King Jesus rules the heavenly realms. As a people called according to His name, we can allow that heavenly Kingdom to rule all believers in Christ Jesus in this earth realm. One way the manifestation of that Kingdom becomes apparent is when we control the money flow through the supernatural power of God. In Deuteronomy 15:6, Moses gives the word of God to all Israel.

*For the Lord your God will bless you just as He prom-
ised you; you shall **lend** to many nations, but you shall
not borrow; you shall **reign** over many nations, but
they shall not reign over you.*

God wants you to rule and reign. He wants you to obtain
wealth because satan desires to control you and control this system
through debt. Here in Deuteronomy, we have the idea that the Lord
wants to bless us. He has promised you different things and wants
to bless you. He says here, concerning the nation of Israel, that they
will lend to many nations, but they will not need to borrow. That
sounds like prosperity to me!

The truth stated here means that we will rule and reign over
nations but they will not prevail over us. That's what Deuteronomy
15:6 is saying. So, it is God's plan for every Christian to prosper to
the point that not one of God's children ever needs to borrow. The
Lord wants to do this openly so that everyone will see. He wants
to display His covenant to everyone through His people. One of
the ways that God confirms this is in how He promises wealth
through the financial system and He promises that wealth to His
children. God intends that only He and no one else will rule over
His children.

With all of this being said, any kind of debt system that tries to
control God's children is wrong. Anything that attempts to exercise
authority over His children is wrong. We have this freedom that
comes into the financial realm from the realms of Heaven.

When God says you are going to lend, then you are not going
to borrow—you are going to reign over nations. Other nations are
going to depend on us because God is with us. The blessing of the
Lord is coming upon His people.

The blessing of the Lord has to do with His covenant. It is a covenant where wealth will come through you and your life, and you will reign over the enemy.

God Will Bless

It is time for the supernatural to invade your finances. When God's realm of the supernatural encounters the natural, to those who yield, blessings will come to the believing ones. Deuteronomy 16:15 says, "The Lord your God will bless you in all your produce and in all the work of your hands, so that you surely rejoice."

The Lord will overcome you with goodness to the point that even the works of your hands will be blessed. When a believer sees this occurring, a shift will happen in their heart. This shift will cause you to have great joy. Everything that you touch will prosper as you enjoy a supernatural invasion in your finances and every part of your life.

God's plan for His people is that we should not lack anything. That is just the way the Lord is. He wants to bless us and to confirm His goodness to us.

Your Way Is Prosperous

> *This Book of the Law* [the Word of God] *shall not depart from your mouth, but you shall meditate in it day and night, that you may observe to do according to all that is written in it. For then you will make your way prosperous, and then you will have good success* (Joshua 1:8).

Here in the book of Joshua we see that it is God's perfect plan that we meditate on His Word, say it with our mouth, and be watchful to do everything that is written. This is going to make our way prosperous. There is a prosperity that is coming to you because you do not depart from the Word of God. You meditate on it and speak it with your mouth. When you observe and do everything that is written in the Word, you will prosper. You will have your way made prosperous. God has assured that you will have good success because this is the promise of the Word of God. There is the process and the example that we should follow that is mentioned in Joshua 1:8: "remember to meditate" on everything that God says. Here is God's will for you every day. We need to put into action all that we believe. God promises to make our way prosperous and give us good success. The Holy Spirit wants to get these things across to us through the revelation of the Word of God.

Seek God

Another essential battle strategy that we must adhere to and implement into our lives is in Second Chronicles 26:

> He [King Uzziah] *sought God in the days of Zechariah, who had understanding in the visions of God; and as long as he sought the Lord, God made him prosper* (2 Chronicles 26:5).

The Bible says King Uzziah sought God in the days of Zechariah. That is a significant activity concerning your participation in *supernatural finances*. The king had understanding in the visions of God, which is a great asset to a leader. However, the key is that as long as he sought the Lord, God made him prosper.

You can understand that God is saying this to us as well—as long as a person continues to have a seeking heart toward the Lord, that person is going to prosper. We need to continue to seek the Lord; then He will come to us in visions and revelations. We will gain an understanding of what God is saying because of the revelation of the Word of God. We have an effective battle strategy where God gives us a supernatural vision. He causes us to know what is going on behind the scenes as well as the future. As long as we continue to seek Him, He is going to continue to prosper us in every area.

Taking Time to Meditate

Blessed is the man [person] *who walks not in the counsel of the ungodly, nor stands in the path of sinners, nor sits in the seat of the scornful; but his delight is in the law of the Lord, and in His law he meditates day and night. He shall be like a tree planted by the rivers of water, that brings forth its fruit in its season, whose leaf also shall not wither; and **whatever he does shall prosper*** (Psalm 1:1-3)

As believers, we need to walk in the counsel of God and not in the counsel of ungodly people who are part of a perverse generation and the corrupt financial system as well. This unbelieving generation is faithless and is referred to by Jesus in dealing with their inability to cast out a demon. "Then Jesus answered and said, 'O faithless and perverse generation, how long shall I be with you and bear with you? Bring your son here'" (Luke 9:41). We need to not sit with the scornful or stand in the path of sinners, but stay separate, standing in faith, believing. We are to delight in the Lord and everything that He has ever said. It is time to meditate day and night on everything that God has written. As a result, a person is going to find themselves like a tree that is planted by the rivers of living water, supernaturally bringing forth fruit in season. That person will not see their life wither in any way but will instead see everything that they put their hands to prosper!

Receive Your Protection

Another battle strategy is the truth that the Lord will be a refuge to His loved ones. We need to remember that our God has a place for us when we are in trouble. We need to seek shelter in Him quickly. As a child of Almighty God, you can run to Him and hide in times of crisis. The supernatural will be activated, and you can be safe. No one's going to touch you in that place. It's a secret place of refuge that He has provided for His precious ones. It's a very high tower, and the Lord will preserve you as His own. Nothing's going to harm you there. "The Lord also will be a refuge and a high tower for the oppressed, a refuge and a stronghold in times of trouble" (Ps. 9:9 AMPC).

Table of Honor

Another battle strategy for supernatural finances is in Psalm 23:

> *The Lord is my shepherd; I shall not want* [I shall not lack anything]. *You prepare a table* [a feast] *before me in the presence of my enemies; You anoint my head with oil; my cup runs over* [in abundance]. *Surely goodness and mercy shall follow me all the days of my life* (Psalm 23:1, 5-6).

The Lord is a good Shepherd, and you don't have anything to fear because He is watching over His beloved. Not only will He give His children everything they need, but they also are not going to want for anything as well. The Lord is going to set the table for them in the presence of their enemies and anoint them with abundance. That abundance will overflow, and God Almighty will have mercy on all who sit at the table. Remember that God is going to flood you with plenty so that you can help others. Supernatural goodness and mercy will follow you all the days of your life, and you will be overtaken and overcome by them for the distribution of *supernatural finances* to others.

God's Pleasure

Another battle strategy for supernatural finances is in Psalm 35:

> *Let them shout for joy and be glad, who favor my righteous cause; and let them say continually, "Let the Lord be magnified, who has pleasure in the prosperity of His servant"* (Psalm 35:27).

We need to understand that God takes pleasure when He prospers one of His servants. How much more His children because of Jesus Christ. According to this psalm, the Lord is the One who gets magnified. He gets all the attention to show Himself faithful. God will reveal Himself faithful and give favor for the righteous cause. If you call out to Him right now, you can receive this favor. He will help you with your finances. Continually magnify Him, and He is going to confirm His covenant with you. If you place your trust in Him, you will have nothing to worry about concerning your life.

Trust God

God desires to prosper you and give you everything that you need. He wants to do this because He takes great pleasure in doing so. In Psalms, it says, "They [those who trust in God] are abundantly satisfied with the fullness of Your house, and You give them drink from the river of Your pleasures" (Ps. 36:8).

This battle strategy is essential because you need to always remember to trust in God. The Almighty is the one who can abundantly satisfy you. Trust in Him and His promises because they are sure. He promises to abundantly fill you with the fullness of His house because you are a child of God and you dwell in His home. God is going to prosper you abundantly, so be sure to thank Him in advance about it. The battle strategies of the Lord concerning supernatural finances are available to you so that you can go to the *river of pleasure* and take a drink. *Supernatural finances* are coming your way because Father God will abundantly supply everything you ask of Him.

Delight in Him

In Psalm 37:3-4 it says, "Trust in the Lord, and do good; dwell in the land [the blessing] and feed on His faithfulness. Delight yourself also in the Lord, and He shall give you the desires of your heart."

In this battle strategy, there is a need to trust in the Lord your God continually. A Christian needs to frequently acknowledge God Almighty in all their ways. He is faithful. We need to think about Jehovah's faithfulness toward us at all times because He loves us so.

Father God is going to take what is His and give it to His children. He takes delight in you and loves you very dearly. Therefore, this is a critical battle strategy for supernatural finances. He is willing to give you the desires of your heart if you allow Him to do so. Just trust in Him. He delights in giving you the desires of your heart, whatever they are. God wants to do this today for you. Just continue to meditate on the truth and let this be your practice every day.

The Lord Knows

The Holy Spirit is wanting you to yield to the promises that He is giving you. Let faith arise in your heart. In Psalm 37:18-19 it says, "The Lord knows the days of the upright, and their inheritance shall be forever. They shall not be ashamed in the evil time, and in the days of famine they shall be satisfied."

We need to remember that God knows all of our days. He is looking over us and watching over us, ready to provide for every need. He's going to keep your inheritance forever that He's giving you.

You are His beloved child, and nothing can stop Him from expressing that love to you. Your future is secure as you walk with Him intimately and you will have nothing to be concerned or worried about in your life. Nothing shall be lost even in a famine. Your inheritance is what the Lord has promised you. This a crucial strategy that God has given us—that we have an eternal inheritance and that God already knows the days that are ahead. He has provided for you ahead of time. You're going to be satisfied even in a famine!

Never Forsaken

The next battle strategy is in Psalm 37:25: "I have been young, and now am old; yet I have not seen the righteous forsaken, nor his descendants begging bread."

Here we have King David, who says that the Lord is watching over him continually. King David says the Lord is never going to leave, so you can be encouraged right now. The Lord watches over your life, and He is never going to leave you because of His faithfulness. God is going to show Himself strong and is coming through for you. Do not allow fear to enter. He is not going to keep you in need much longer. He is going to provide for you. When He comes, He will give supernatural finances to you. It is going to be a mighty deliverance that God has for His children through the Holy Spirit.

I want you to know that the Lord has come to help you, to reveal the love of God the Father to you. The Holy Spirit is saying that His children have nothing to worry about concerning their lives.

Chosen

The next battle strategy is in Psalm 65:4. The psalmist says, "Blessed is the man You choose, and cause to approach You, that he may dwell in Your courts. We shall be satisfied with the goodness of Your house, of Your holy temple."

Here we see that the Lord is inviting us into His courts. Here is another battle strategy—we have been given access to the Holy of Holies through Christ Jesus. He is the New and Living Way. Jesus has made the way by His blood. He has allowed the veil to be torn and has given us access to His throne through the blood of Jesus. God now considers us His children, and as children we need to regularly go into the House of the Lord and behold His goodness. We are invited by the Lord to dwell in the courts of our God. The Lord wants us to be satisfied with every good thing.

Paths of Abundance

The next battle strategy is in Psalm 65. It says, "You crown the year with Your goodness, and Your paths drip with abundance (Ps. 65:11).

The path that the Lord has chosen for us is a path that will prosper. It is the path that He desires for us according to His knowledge and plans. Those plans drip with abundance so that we can encounter supernatural overflow in our life, according to Scripture. The Holy Spirit wants to lead you into all truth. He wants you to experience this abundance. The Lord has chosen a path for us that is prosperous.

A Wealthy Place

Another battle strategy for supernatural finances is "a wealthy place." It says in Psalm 66:12, "We went through fire and through water; but You brought us out to rich fulfillment" (KJV: "wealthy place").

Whatever it is that you are going through or have gone through, either past or present, God wants you to know that He was with you. He's going to bring you out into a prosperous place now that you have passed all of your tests. Now, God trusts you. He is faithful to deliver you from all your troubles, and it will be well worth it when you see the deliverance that God Almighty is bringing in your life.

Rest assured that God is with you and that He has plans for you. He has not forgotten you. He is going to prove His faithfulness to you. The trouble that you went through is going to be well worth it.

God Sets You

The next battle strategy is in Psalm 68:6: "God sets the solitary in families; He brings out those who are bound into prosperity; but the rebellious dwell in a dry land."

Here we observe that the strategies God has given us for supernatural finances are the following:

1. The Lord has adopted you, and we have this spirit of adoption according to Romans 8:15. The apostle Paul said that the Spirit of God within us is crying out "Abba Father" because we are adopted. You are a child of God. You've taken on God's name and have all the benefits of being in the household of God.

2. The Lord takes you out of bondage and places you into His family.

3. You are loved, and Your Father brings you out of poverty into prosperity just like the psalmist says. You are not bound anymore. The Spirit has ushered you into freedom. The deliverance for your life has come, and now you are in the family of God. It is going to go well with you because *God has set you.*

Loading Us with Benefits

The next battle strategy is *loading us with benefits.* In Psalm 68:19, it says, "Blessed be the Lord, who daily loads us with benefits, the God of our salvation!" We need to understand the Lord Himself is going to reward a Christian for their faithfulness to Him. He has kept track of everything you have done for Him. He has watched over us and now He knows that He can trust you. Because of this fact, He is going to load that person down with all kinds of benefits. In this scripture the heart of the Lord is revealed and what He desires for you.

Father God wants to prosper you and have you full of His abundance. A Christian is not going to need to worry anymore because according to Psalm 68 they are blessed.

Father God loads you with benefits, daily. The Lord is powerful and is a God of deliverance. He is a God of salvation and a God of abundant provision.

Good Things

The next battle strategy we want to talk about concerning supernatural finances is in Psalm 84: "For the Lord God is a sun and shield; the Lord will give grace and glory; no good thing will He withhold from those who walk uprightly" (Ps. 84:11).

The Lord is a Protector. He is continually making the way bright for the believer. The Lord is going to give you grace and reveal His glory. No good thing does He withhold from the believer. There is a need to meditate on the truth that God is not limiting you. We meditate on the fact that walking upright before Him will cause Him to not hold anything back from us as His beloved child. It is time to experience His glory and mercy. The Almighty is not going to hide Himself any longer. He will come and show Himself to you.

You have been deemed faithful,
and God will walk with you.

Multiply Greatly

You are going to prosper according to Psalm 107:38: "He also blesses them, and they multiply greatly; and He does not let their cattle decrease."

Another powerful strategy is the fact that the Lord's going to continually bless His children and allow them to multiply in His Kingdom. Here is an example of the personality and the ways of

God. He does not decrease but only increases. The truth is, everything will grow in a believer's life. Even to where the Scripture says that your cattle will increase and not fail. Everything about your life is going to increase. That is the way that God works according to the Scriptures.

> God's battle strategy for supernatural finances is that you are going to multiply. You can be blessed and are going to increase. So, you need to meditate on these things because that is what God intends for you. The Lord will profoundly come into your life and provide for you through His strategies in His Word.

The Bright Path

But the path of the just is like the shining sun, that shines ever brighter unto the perfect day (Proverbs 4:18).

As we continue to consistently walk with the Lord, the results will be apparent. Your path will become brighter and brighter, for this is God's plan for you. According to Proverbs, we have a path that we are walking on as believers. We are going to shine like the sun because the path of the just is shining like the sun. The perfect day of the Lord is leading you into the brightness of His glory. Supernatural encounters in the glory are in store for those who choose His path. The Lord has His perfect day as your destination.

He has plans for you to prosper and He will securely lead you into this glorious time of supernatural finances.

Restoration

Another battle strategy is *restoration* found in Proverbs 6. King Solomon says, "People do not despise a thief if he steals to satisfy himself when he is starving. Yet when he is found, he must restore sevenfold" (Prov. 6:30-31).

If the enemy stole from you and then was caught, he must pay back sevenfold. That is what the Scripture teaches. So it is with satan—he must pay you back where anything has been stolen and restore to you seven times over when caught. Therefore, you need to let the Spirit of God show you what satan is doing. Then you need to declare that the thief is exposed. Then you need to demand that he repay sevenfold. The Lord Himself is going to take up your case. Those of you who have been stolen from, the battle strategy is that Jehovah is going to bring restoration and recompense. So not only is He going to restore the stolen goods, but repayment is the idea of the sevenfold return on the stolen goods to close the case in your favor!

God will make sure there is a provision for you. God is going to come through. Just continue to meditate on Proverbs 6:30, because the Lord God is going to bring you restoration and recompense.

Full Treasuries

That I may cause those who love me to inherit wealth,
that I may fill their treasuries (Proverbs 8:21).

Now, this is a beautiful scripture because the Lord is saying through the wisdom contained in Proverbs that He is going to cause those who love wisdom to inherit wealth that they may fill their treasuries. The Lord is going to generate wealth to come to you, and He is going to fill your treasuries because you love Him.

 Because you asked for wisdom, God says, "I'm going to provide for you and fill your treasuries and your storehouses!"

No Lack

Another battle strategy is in Proverbs 10:3: "The Lord will not allow the righteous soul to famish."

In this battle strategy, our Father is reminding us that He is watching over all. He is concerned about those who love Him. Jesus Christ has made the believer righteous in His sight. God, your Father, is with you in a mighty way and Jesus's blood has allowed you to become righteous. The Father is not going to let your soul experience lack for long because He is going to restore you. Remember to meditate on this battle strategy concerning supernatural finances.

The Lord's going to restore you. Even your soul, not just your spirit, is going to be restored. That is what He wants to do by His power. He desires to deliver you; He desires to revive you. You are not going to be famished very long because God is your Provider.

Rich with No Sorrow

Another battle strategy is in Proverbs 10:22 which says, "The blessing of the Lord makes one rich, and He adds no sorrow with it."

In this proverb, the Lord is desiring to prosper His children to bless them. Our heavenly Father wants to make them rich. Any earthly father who genuinely loves his children wants to provide for them. That's what it says here in the Scriptures.

He blesses people, and He makes them wealthy. However, when He does this, the promise is that no sadness or curse is going to come with it. Instead, only a joy unspeakable. God, who is a loving heavenly Father, is going to overwhelm His children with joy as well.

It's not just about the prosperity or being rich. It's the fact that God wants to provide for you and for you encounter joy, not sorrow. God is with you in a mighty way.

Desires Granted

> *The fear of the wicked will come upon him, and the desire of the righteous will be granted* (Proverbs 10:24).

Remember that whatever the wicked fears is going to come upon them, but the perfect love of God drives out fear in your life. Your heavenly Father will grant you the desires of your heart because Christ Jesus has made you the righteousness of God. What is the Holy Spirit saying to you concerning what comes upon those who are wicked, as compared to what comes upon those with perfect love? The Holy Spirit is saying to you that God is granting the desires of your heart because you have been made righteous by the blood of Jesus Christ.

The Generous Will Prosper

Just get excited, because God is making a way to provide for us through another battle strategy located in Proverbs 11:

> *A generous person will prosper; whoever refreshes others will be refreshed* (Proverbs 11:25 NIV).

A generous man will always prosper because he helps replenish others. A Christian will continually be refreshed if they implement this battle strategy. The idea is that you cannot out-give God, so when God tells you to give to someone, He is honestly setting you up for a "supernatural finance" encounter. We need to be generous at all times. Being generous is something that we must learn and must permit the Lord to heal us of any hurts preventing us from showing generosity. A generous person will prosper when you refresh someone. You can expect that God is going to come and restore the supernatural provision you refreshed someone with.

The Lord is going to do it, and it will be a supernatural encounter with God.

Inheritance

Another battle strategy is in Proverbs 13:22: "A good man leaves an inheritance to his children's children, but the wealth of the sinner is stored up for the righteous."

A good man is one who prospers enough to leave wealth for a couple of generations. So, this is not just for us; it is for those who come after us. God desires that a Christian be wealthy so that they can leave an inheritance. Remember this: a sinner is hard at work piling up money and wealth for the Christian. So, remember, this battle strategy contains the truth that a Christian should allow God to prosper them so that other generations can also flourish.

You see, everything on the earth is not in submission to God as of yet. We must bring correction to that which is not submitted by speaking and demanding evil forces to yield to God's will. Placing a demand causes a release of the Kingdom of God into the situation, whatever it might be. Mark 11:23-26 is one of the earthly assignments that I have been charged to teach and live by:

> For assuredly, I say to you, whoever says to this mountain, "Be removed and be cast into the sea," and does not doubt in his heart, but believes that those things he says will be done, he will have whatever he says. Therefore I say to you, whatever things you ask when you pray, believe that you receive them, and you will have them.
>
> And whenever you stand praying, if you have anything against anyone, forgive him, that your Father in

*heaven may also forgive you your trespasses. But if you
do not forgive, neither will your Father in heaven forgive your trespasses.*

The fact is, every believer is called to live the life described in these verses. More than you can even imagine is possible for you if you will only believe that the things you say will be done.

I remember when my wife and I started practicing the verses concerning speaking to a mountain. We decided that God wanted us to become debt-free, so we started talking to our debt mountain. From 2000 to 2008, we proclaimed that we were debt-free and commanded debt to get out. Soon our debt began to disappear. In 2008, the only debt we had left was our mortgage payment. Obviously, we were careful not to create more debt and did everything we could in the natural to pay off the debt, but we also received supernatural assistance.

At that point, the Lord told me to pay a person's mortgage payment for them. I remember thinking that I would never pay off our own mortgage if we kept handing out money to others to pay theirs. Actually, in a way, I was right. We didn't pay off our mortgage— God did! Someone left us enough money in a will to pay off our mortgage in February of 2008.

Speak to your mountains! God's Word does perform just as He says it will. God would not have put those verses in the Bible if He did not want us to practice them.

In Mark 9:23, Jesus said, "If you can believe, all things are possible to him who believes." So what is the problem? Why are we not seeing this truth manifested in our lives as it should be?

The fact is that we need to be diligent in our daily lives by walking in love and forgiveness. When we neglect these two very

important character traits, we can hinder our faith and find ourselves ineffective in moving our mountains.

Chapter 4

ACCESSING BATTLE STRATEGIES CONCERNING GIVING AND RECEIVING: PART TWO

The House of the Righteous

The next battle strategy is in Proverbs 15:6: "In the house of the righteous there is much treasure: but in the revenue of the wicked is trouble."

In this battle strategy regarding supernatural finances, we have the fact that the blood of Jesus has made us righteous in the sight of God. We are the righteousness of God in Christ Jesus. This scripture says that the house of the righteous has much treasure and we are the righteousness of God through Jesus Christ, so our houses are to be full of wealth. God is with us, and He is in our house.

Therefore, no trouble shall follow and we don't have to worry about anything. God is going to be with us in a mighty way.

Humility and the Fear of the Lord

The next battle strategy is Proverbs 22:4: "By humility and the fear of the Lord [worship and reverence] are riches and honor and life."

I want you to know the love of the Lord God and His desire to give you riches, honor, and life. By humbling ourselves in His glory, we reverence and worship Him. We need to allow Him to overcome us as we worship Him, humbling ourselves before the Lord and He will surely lift us and promote us.

By humility and the fear of the Lord, we receive riches, honor, and life. We need to bow before Him continually. We need to implement reverence and humility in our lives. We need to fear the Lord, and He will promote us. He is going to lift you up in due season. You have nothing to worry about because He is with you.

Love the Lord by humbling yourself in reverence and worship before Him. The Lord will surely lift you up and promote you. He desires to give you riches, honor, and life.

Good Things

The next battle strategy is in Proverbs 28:10: "Whoso causeth the righteous to go astray in an evil way, he shall fall himself into his own pit: but the upright shall have good things in possession" (KJV).

The Lord is going to guide and protect you. With this guidance and protection, you are not going to need to fear anything. God is with you because you're upright and you fear the Lord. Therefore, you are going to have all good things in your possession. God is going to be so good that you can have good things coming from a good God and they're going to be yours. God is going to overwhelm you with His goodness, but you have nothing to fear.

God is with you, and He is protecting you right now.

The Lord will guide and protect you. You have nothing to fear. Because you are upright, you will have good things in your possession.

Abounding with Blessings

The next battle strategy is in Proverbs 28:20: "A faithful man will abound with blessings."

If you are faithful to the Lord, He is going to reward you, but you need to understand and accept this. You have nothing to fear. You are going to abound with blessings according to this proverb. There are rewards for those who are faithful. Rewards and blessings are coming to you!

You are faithful, and He will reward you. You will abound with blessings.

Trust Brings Prosperity

The next battle strategy is in Proverbs 28:25: "He who is of a proud heart stirs up strife, but he who trusts in the Lord will be prospered."

We need to rely heavily on the Lord, and He will prosper us because we trust in Him. In your relationship with God, allow that trust to come forth continually and do not yield to fear or doubt. Don't let strife be stirred up but continuously remain humble in the sight of the Almighty and He is going to prosper you.

Continually trust the Lord and see Him flourish you. Do not allow strife to be stirred up, but instead always remain humble in the sight of Almighty God.

The Gift of God

The next battle strategy is in Ecclesiastes 5:19: "As for every man to whom God has given riches and wealth, and given him power to eat of it, to receive his heritage and rejoice in his labor—this is the gift of God."

In this battle strategy, we must remember that God gives us the power to obtain wealth. God has given you the ability to acquire wealth and desires for you to rejoice in this gift that He has given you.

So, acknowledge Him in all your ways and remember that it is God who gives you the power to obtain riches and wealth. He wants us to give Him recognition for it. It's a gift of God.

Willing and Obedient

The next battle strategy in Isaiah 1:19 says, "If you are willing and obedient, you shall eat the good [the best] of the land."

The best of the land is the next battle strategy for supernatural finances. It is the fact that we need to acknowledge that God is guiding us along the way and that He desires for us to obey His instructions. When the Lord God gives you instructions, you have to realize that those instructions are going to lead you into a wealthy and prosperous place. Because God does not think about losing anything, He doesn't think about the things that we think about. He has good plans and a good ending plan for you. This obedience will allow you to participate in the best or the wealthiest places in the land.

The Holy Spirit wants to guide you into these places. He wants to teach you and guide you along the way. So we're just going to yield to Him and allow Him to do this. It's an essential battle strategy.

Plenteous

The next battle strategy is in Isaiah 30:23: "Then He will give the rain for your seed with which you sow the ground, and bread of the increase of the earth; it will be fat and plentiful. In that day your cattle will feed in large pastures."

In this battle strategy, these are the things that you need to understand:

1. God is a God of increase in your life, so He always wants you to increase.

2. He wants you to have rain in seasons so that the seed that you have sown will cause an increase.

3. You will be plenteous in everything—even your cattle are going to feed in large pastures.

Whatever you can trust God for, He's going to provide for you. You simply need to trust Him for your provision. We need to look to Him for that supernatural provision from Heaven.

> Supernatural finances are going to come to you. The increase is occurring in your life. Whatever you can trust God for, He will provide.

A New Thing

The next battle strategy from Heaven is Isaiah 43:18-21: "Do not remember the former things, nor consider the things of old. Behold, I will do a new thing, now it shall spring forth; shall you not know it? I will even make a road in the wilderness and rivers in the desert...to give drink to My people, My chosen. This people I have formed for Myself; they shall declare My praise."

This battle strategy for supernatural finances is that you need to remember that you are chosen—you are God's chosen son or daughter. You are God ordained, you are called, and God has chosen you in this generation.

Your loving heavenly Father has amazing plans for you. You need to see that there are rivers of water coming through the desert of your life right now. God is bringing prosperity your way and He is making streams appear in the desert. He has made you because He thought of you and placed you in your mother's womb. Now, He has brought you to this place for Himself.

He is going to give you all the things that you would ever desire from the springs of living water that are coming forth. Continue to worship Him. He wants you to forget the past. Just continue to worship Him and enjoy what is happening because God is coming through for you.

Things to remember:

1. You are God's chosen.

2. Your loving heavenly Father has awesome plans for you.

3. He can even make rivers appear in the desert.

4. He has formed you for Himself.

5. We will give Him praise for all that He has done when the new springs forth.

6. He wants you to forget the past and enjoy what is coming.

Riches of Secret Places

The next battle strategy for supernatural finances is in Isaiah 45:2-3:

> *I will go before you and level the mountains [to make the crooked places straight]; I will break in pieces the doors of bronze and cut asunder the bars of iron. And I will give you the treasures of darkness and hidden*

riches of secret places, that you may know that it is I, the Lord, the God of Israel, Who calls you by your name (AMPC).

In this battle strategy for supernatural finances, we see the Lord Himself desires to see you free. He desires for you to experience deliverance entirely, so He is coming to help you. He has promised to break the bars that imprison you and to show you the secret treasures and where they are located.

There are secret places that you don't know of, but God knows where they are. He is going to help you because He calls you by name. The Holy Spirit is with you along with His intervention on your behalf as you follow His direction, His provision, and His revelation of hidden treasures in secret places. It is His desire for you to know this.

> The Lord teaches us to profit. He will lead you into all truth and prosper you in the way chosen for you.

God Teaches You to Profit

The next battle strategy in Isaiah 48:17 says, "Thus says the Lord, your Redeemer, the Holy One of Israel: 'I am the Lord your God, who teaches you to profit, who leads you by the way you should go.'"

According to this scripture, it says that the Lord teaches us how to profit and leads us in the way that we should go. It is comforting to know that He is leading us. He is the way of truth and the way of prosperity. The Lord has chosen this path for you according to this scripture.

The battle strategy is to meditate on the power of God and how He has placed us on a path where we are on a road of truth. He has a plan to prosper us in this way that God has chosen for us.

Joy and Gladness

The next battle strategy in Isaiah 51:3 says, "For the Lord will comfort Zion, He will comfort [pity, change] all her waste places; He will make her wilderness like Eden, and her desert like the garden of the Lord; joy and gladness will be found in it, thanksgiving and the voice of melody."

This battle strategy is essential because we need to understand that our heavenly Father, according to this scripture, is wanting to comfort us. He is reassuring us in all the things that we go through. He is ready to perform a miracle and cause us to flourish like the garden of God.

Here is what the Holy Spirit is saying to us: "Your heavenly Father comforts you. He will perform a miracle and cause you to flourish like the garden of God. Joy shall come as you give thanks for His faithfulness."

The Lord Guides You

The next battle strategy in Isaiah 58:11 says, "The Lord will guide you continually, and satisfy your soul in drought, and strengthen your bones; you shall be like a watered garden, and like a spring of water, whose waters do not fail."

In this battle strategy, we are reminded once again that the Lord is going to guide us. He is going to guide you and me continually without any interruption. He is going to satisfy our soul even in the dry times of our lives and strengthen our bodies. We are going to be like a well-watered garden, like a spring of water that is not going to fail so that you we have a continual flow.

God is with you forever, so you need to be encouraged because the power of the Holy Spirit is ministering to you right now. God's will for your life is that He wants to you to flourish. The Lord is going to give you supernatural finances to help get you on track with what He has for you. The Lord promises to guide you continually and defeat your enemy.

I Know Your Thoughts

God has thoughts of peace and not of evil to give you a future and hope in this battle strategy in Jeremiah 29:11: "For I know the thoughts that I think toward you, says the Lord, thoughts of peace and not of evil, to give you a future and a hope."

The Lord says to you, "I know the thoughts that I think toward you." We have to understand that God has thoughts toward us that are good. In fact, as a child of His, He doesn't think evil thoughts toward you. God wants to go a step further with more than dreams. He plans on making them a reality.

He has plans for you. Those plans include supernatural finances and the fact that we are going to succeed. Always remember that God's plans are to prosper you and cause you to flourish.

He has thoughts of peace and nothing evil. God has not planned anything evil to happen to you.

Goodness and Prosperity

Jeremiah 33 contains the next battle strategy:

Then it shall be to Me a name of joy, a praise, and an honor before all nations of the earth, who shall hear all the good that I do to them; they shall fear and tremble for all the goodness and all the prosperity that I provide for it (Jeremiah 33:9).

This battle strategy is crucial because:

1. God loves us.

2. He loves to advertise His goodness to the nations.

3. He will pour out His love and goodness on us just so the countries can see it.

4. He wants to have His name known.

5. He wants to prosper His people and provide for them.

However, He does all this to confirm His covenant and to show the nations of the world that He loves His people. It is to provoke people to jealousy. That is a battle strategy where God is working through His own. His children are to display His prosperity to help those people on the outside to see that He is a good God. So, let Him advertise His goodness to the nations as He prospers and provides for you.

> He's going to deliver you from your situations; repayment is coming from the enemy for what he has stolen from you. Satan is going to have to pay it back.

Restoration

The next battle strategy in Joel 2:25-26 says:

> *So I will restore to you the years that the swarming locust has eaten, the crawling locust, the consuming locust, and the chewing locust. ...You shall eat in plenty and be satisfied, and praise the name of the Lord your God, who has dealt wondrously with you; and My people shall never be put to shame.*

This battle strategy instructs you to allow God to speak to you that He is a God of restoration. He wants to take everything you've gone through and make it up to you. He wants to go back and start to restore parts of your life that you might have even forgotten. God is a God of restoration, and supernatural finances will bring renewal. The next thing the Lord wants to do is to repay you for what the enemy has stolen from you. He wants to deal wondrously with you. Your heavenly Father can make it better for you. He is also not going to allow you to be put to shame ever again.

Assets

The next battle strategy in Haggai 2:8 says, "'The silver is Mine, and the gold is Mine,' says the Lord of hosts."

God makes it clear that those precious metals that He has placed on the earth are His. Your God is wealthy and owns precious metals. As God is our heavenly Father, we inherit all these things from God, and He wants to do good things for us. Remember this battle strategy even though this world used to be God's and He has made it for man. He still owns the silver and the gold.

> Your heavenly Father God is rich and holds the precious metals of the earth.

Possess All Things

The next battle strategy is in Zechariah 8:12: "For the seed shall be prosperous, the vine shall give its fruit, the ground shall give her increase, and the heavens shall give their dew—I will cause the remnant of this people to possess all these."

Now, in this battle strategy remember that increase is coming to you in every way. You are going to be prosperous in everything you do because of the heavens being released to you whether it be on the ground, on the vine, or in the heavens. According to this scripture, God is going to cause the remnant to possess all things. We live in an exceptional time. We are to increase in every way, for we are His special children and will own all things.

The Holy Spirit is saying to you that increase is coming concerning the prosperity of your seed, the fruit of your vine, the increase of the ground, the dew of Heaven, and His children's possession of these things.

Those people who fear the name of the Lord are going to encounter supernatural healing.

Healing in His Wings

The next battle strategy in Malachi 4:2 says, "But to you who fear My name [worship] the Sun of Righteousness shall arise with healing in His wings; and you shall go out and grow fat like stall-fed calves."

The fear of His name will bring reverence. There is a Sun of righteousness with rays of light rising named Jesus that is going to increase with healing. Your healing is coming, and you're going to be restored and healed. God is going to give you the desires of your heart.

Seek First

Another battle strategy in Matthew 6:33 says, "But seek first the kingdom of God and His righteousness, and all these things shall be added to you."

This strategy concerns those who are seeking the Kingdom of God first and foremost. The priority is not to seek out wealth but to seek after God's Kingdom and the wealth will come to you.

Do this and God is going to ensure that you have all you need. Our God is loving and righteous. He is going to give you everything that your heart desires. If you seek after His righteousness, He is going to provide all things for you. We have His attention.

> Seek God's Kingdom first, and you will see that God will ensure you have all you need. He is righteous, and you are to seek His righteousness with all your heart. As you continually seek the Lord, He will never fail to provide all things for you.

Good Gifts

The next battle strategy in Matthew 7:11 says, "If you then, being evil, know how to give good gifts to your children, how much more will your Father who is in heaven give good things to those who ask Him!"

Your heavenly Father knows and loves you and wants to give you good gifts. He already knows what you need and is willing to provide you with the best gifts. No earthly father could exceed the heavenly Father in giving, so remember that and meditate on this strategy from Heaven. Meditate on the fact that the heavenly Father loves you and wants to provide you with all good things.

There is a reward system for all that you give up to follow Jesus. In this life, you will receive a hundredfold. As well as all the good things, persecutions will come for this abundance and reward that you receive in this present life.

Receive One Hundredfold

The next battle strategy is in Mark 10:28-30:

> *Then Peter began to say to Him, "See, we have left all and followed You." So Jesus answered and said, "Assuredly, I say to you, there is no one who has left house or brothers or sisters or father or mother or wife or children or lands, for My sake and the gospel's, who shall not receive a hundredfold now in this time— houses and brothers and sisters and mothers and children and lands, with persecutions—and in the age to come, eternal life."*

This battle strategy for supernatural finances is essential as well because it talks about a reward system that God has. There is a reward system for all that you give up to follow Jesus in this life. You are going to receive a hundredfold return, according to this scripture in Matthew, as well as all the good things God gives. You're also going to be persecuted for the abundance that is coming your way. You're going to receive rewards in this life as well as in the next. If there are persecutions, so be it. Be sure to meditate on these scriptures because God wants to provide for you in every way. However, this verse says there's also going to be persecution because of it.

Give and Receive

The next battle strategy for supernatural finances is in Luke 6:38. Jesus said, "Give, and it will be given to you: good measure, pressed down, shaken together, and running over will be put into your bosom. For with the same measure that you use, it will be measured back to you."

God has not forgotten all the gifts that you have given Him. He is going to reward you according to how you have measured it out. If you are continually generous, then He is always going to be generous. Remember that supernatural finances involve taking what is from the heavenly realm and distributing them after they physically manifest on the earth. Through faith, we can obtain these things by believing God and yielding to Him by our willingness to give.

We give, and we know that it is going to be given to us. The battle strategy is that good measure, pressed down, shaken together, and running over will come back into your bosom.

Give You the Kingdom

The next battle strategy in Luke 12:32 says, "Do not fear, little flock, for it is your Father's good pleasure to give you the kingdom."

We have a battle strategy that says, "Do not fear." God our Father is going to give us the Kingdom; it is pleasure! Remember to meditate on this truth that God is going to give you the Kingdom because He desires to. The Lord is excited for the provision that's coming to you, so don't fear because you are going to see your deliverance.

Let the truth of God rule and reign in your life. The truth will set you free from any bondage.

Truth Brings Freedom

The next battle strategy in John 8:32 says, "And you shall know the truth, and the truth shall make you free."

Now is the time to let the truth of God rule and reign in your life. Part of that truth concerns supernatural finances. You desire to know the truth from Heaven, so you need to receive it from Heaven. However, the reality is that you need to see the manifestation in this physical realm as well. God is commanding the release to come. The truth is going to set you free from any bondage. Part of that bondage in this physical realm would be debt, so you are going to become debt-free because the Spirit of Truth will not allow you to be ensnared or in bondage to anything. Jesus and the Holy Spirit are deliverers, and they are going to give you the truth and it is going to set you free. The revelation of supernatural finances is a part of God taking the truth about something from Heaven and making it known to you. God will cause an increase to come in.

Abundant Life

In John 10:10 we read about the next battle strategy:

> *The thief does not come except to steal, and to kill, and to destroy. I [Jesus] have come that they may have life, and that they may have it more abundantly.*

In this battle strategy, you need to label the enemy by his fruit and by his mission. We know that the enemy is working when we see stealing, killing, and destroying going on. That is how we identify the thief. Jesus only desired to destroy the works of the devil. That is what Jesus came to do. Jesus came and did His work so that satan cannot destroy you. However, Jesus repurchased you for the Father because He wanted His family back. Because you are a child of God, He is going to work through you to enforce the blessing down here. Father God has sent Jesus to give you life and that life more abundantly. Jesus's mission included a provision of abundant life for His people, so you have an inheritance of abundant life. Jesus is working in you and causing abundant life to flow out of you. It is time to label the enemy by the fruit and his mission.

Satan only wishes to destroy you as a child of God. Jesus is greater and came to give you abundant life.

You Will Receive

The next battle strategy is in John 16:23-24:

And in that day you will ask Me nothing. Most assuredly, I say to you, whatever you ask the Father in My name He will give you. Until now you have asked nothing in My name. Ask, and you will receive, that your joy may be full.

Here in this battle strategy concerning supernatural finances Jesus clearly says that we can ask anything, and we are going to receive it. You need to receive right now in your heart and allow God to begin His work on your finances. God is going to give you the desires of your heart.

God is a good God and is going to provide you with what you asked. Receive it. The whole idea here is that the Father wants to give you the Kingdom and have your joy to the full! Jesus clearly says that we can ask anything and we will receive it.

The Holy Spirit is telling you to ask Him for anything and the resulting joy will come.

Heirs of God

The next battle strategy in supernatural finances is in Romans 8:16-17: "The Spirit Himself bears witness with our spirit that we are children of God, and if children, then heirs—heirs of God and joint heirs with Christ, if indeed we suffer with Him, that we may also be glorified together."

These verses are talking about the Holy Spirit and what He does in the operation of the supernatural in your life. The Holy Spirit Himself testifies in our spirit that we are God's children. As children then, we inherit all that God has if we suffer with Him as well. It is exciting to know that we will be glorified together as a result of this. In this battle strategy in Romans, we need to understand that we have the Holy Spirit within us and that He is continually speaking to as we are God's children and He is our heavenly Father. He is telling us that we are joint heirs with Jesus because Jesus bought us.

Freely Give

The next battle strategy in Romans 8:32 says, "He who did not spare His own Son, but delivered Him up for us all, how shall He not with Him also freely give us all things?"

In this battle strategy, we have to remember that God has not withheld His Son from us but has given us His Son. God delivered us through Jesus. He was delivered up and became a sacrifice for us in our place. If we receive Jesus and what He did, then we accept all the good things that come from what Jesus paid for.

> He will not withhold any good thing but will give us all things.

Put Aside As You Have Prospered

> On the first [day] of each week, let each one of you [personally] put aside something and save it up as he has prospered [in proportion to what he is given], so that no collections will need to be taken after I come (1 Corinthians 16:2 AMPC).

Here is the next battle strategy for supernatural finances. The apostle Paul is saying that people have prospered during the week and there is a portion that needs to be set aside to be a gift to God.

Paul is assuming that people have prospered and that they now need to give. He is asking the churches to do this before He comes so that people don't feel like they have to give.

The point here in this battle strategy is that Paul said they should put aside something and save it up as they have prospered. That word *prospered* means to increase. It is according to how God had prospered them or increased them. This battle strategy is essential to understand.

Paul had the church set aside the offerings in advance for his collection when he came. It was according to how much God had "prospered" them.

 Let God increase you so that you can honor Him with an offering from how He has prospered you.

Jesus Is Wealthy

The next battle strategy in Second Corinthians 8:9 says, "For you know the grace of our Lord Jesus Christ, that though He was rich, yet for your sakes He became poor, that you through His poverty might become rich."

In this battle strategy, we need to understand and consider that God sent Jesus back from the wealthiest place in creation to a fallen world. He redeemed us back by the blood of Jesus so that we could become like Him in glory. Because He became poor, He was able to purchase us that we might become rich. We are rich in every single way. God wants to prosper us, not only spiritually but He wants to prosper us supernaturally in our finances. We must accept the fact that He has spiritual and physical blessings.

Spiritual Prosperity

The next battle strategy in Ephesians 1:3 says, "Blessed be the God and Father of our Lord Jesus Christ, who has blessed [prospered] us with every spiritual blessing in the heavenly places in Christ."

In this battle strategy remember that our heavenly Father has blessed us with every spiritual blessing that is in the heavenly realms. However, we are never to doubt that He wants us to grow and mature spiritually and physically in this earthly realm so that everything that we place our hand on will prosper.

Abundantly Above All

The next battle strategy for supernatural finances in Ephesians 3:20 says, "Now to Him who is able to do exceedingly abundantly above all that we ask or think, according to the power that works in us."

God can exceed your expectations with whatever it is that you think He could do. He can do more. It hasn't even entered our mind the things that God has in store for us, but it has been given to us by revelation through the Spirit of God. Jesus Himself has told us to use His name to the Father. There is a mighty power working in us by the Holy Spirit and He is the same Spirit who rose Jesus from the dead.

He is able to do exceedingly and abundantly above all that we could ever ask or think. He is capable of overcoming any fear and any lack in our lives. We are not capable of asking or thinking what God can do for us, so we need to remember that our finite minds limit us, but God wants to reveal these supernatural things by His Spirit.

God can exceed your expectations.
His great power is working in you.

Liberal Supply

The next battle strategy for supernatural finances is in Philippians 4:19: "And my God will liberally supply (fill to the full) your every need according to His riches in glory in Christ Jesus" (AMPC).

In this battle strategy, we need to remember that God has an abundant supply to help you in your life. The Lord wants to show Himself powerful in your time of need. The mighty Holy Spirit wants to fill you up to overflowing so that you can be full, all the time. God, your Father, wants to supply your every need liberally. Every need will be met through Jesus Christ, so trust in Him with your finances. God wants to do this for you. It is according to His riches in the glory that He gives to you. We share in that glory according to Jesus (see John 17).

Every need is fulfilled. Just remember this is an essential battle strategy— there is an abundant supply and there is no lack in Heaven.

No Lack

The next battle strategy is mentioned in First Thessalonians 4:12: "That you may walk properly toward those who are outside, and that you may lack nothing."

God, in this particular battle strategy for supernatural finances, is telling us that we need to walk appropriately in front of the world. The Lord desires us to display His righteousness in our lives. The Lord wants the world and those who are not in HIs Kingdom to be a witness of His goodness.

The Lord wants to have a demonstration of supernatural finances in your life. He wants provision to happen in your life so that other people can see that God takes care of His own. He wants you to lack nothing.

The Holy Spirit is saying to you concerning your walk in this world toward those who do not yet belong to His Kingdom: *Let My provision flow so that My children lack absolutely no good thing!*

Godliness Is Profitable

The next battle strategy in First Timothy 4:8 says, "For bodily exercise profits a little, but godliness is profitable for all things, having promise of the life that now is and of that which is to come."

We need to remember in this battle strategy that godliness is profitable for everything. There is nothing impossible with God, so He wants us to profit. However, godliness is profitable for everything in this present life as well as in the life to come.

We must emphasize this battle strategy of godliness and begin to be imitators of God as dearly loved children (see Eph. 5:1).

There are characteristic traits that Christians should represent of our Father. We should be like Him. We should manifest His character.

Inherit the Promises

The next battle strategy in Hebrews 6:12 says, "Do not become sluggish [lazy], but imitate those who through faith and patience inherit the promises."

In this battle strategy, we need to understand that we are soldiers of Christ. To be good soldiers, and we must not be lazy. We must learn that we are living our lives in front of the world where people are looking at us. We must model our lives after those who inherit the promises through faith and patience. In doing so, we are also going to inherit the promises of God.

Doers of the Word

The next battle strategy in James 1:25 says, "But he who looks into the perfect law of liberty and continues in it, and is not a forgetful hearer but a doer of the word, this one will be blessed in what he does."

In this battle strategy we need to understand that the Word of God is of utmost importance. We also need to continue to look into the Word of God. Just like they looked into the law of Moses back in the Old Testament, we continue to look into the Word of God today.

We need to understand that the Word of God gives us freedom and that freedom is what sets us apart because people are bound all around us. However, when we walk in freedom, we are displaying God's goodness. We must always remember what is given to us by the Word of God and diligently practice the perfect law of liberty. So, the blessing comes because we do what He told us to do.

Prosper in All Things

The next battle strategy in Third John 2 says, "Beloved, I pray that you may prosper in all things and be in health, just as your soul prospers."

Here in this battle strategy we need to remember that the Lord is willing to prosper us. God wants to prosper us in all areas of our lives. The Lord wants us to thrive in our health, our finances, and in our soul.

I have had several substantial financial miracles happen to me as a result of words. Upon graduating from high school, I gave my life to Christ. At that time, I sincerely felt that I wanted to give everything to Him. At a church service shortly after my salvation experience, I wrote a check to the church for every penny I had. I felt that this would express my total commitment to the Lord. I told Him that I would never worry about finances again because He now had all my money.

A year later, I went away to college with only a $100 bill in my pocket that I had received from a senior woman at a prayer meeting I had attended. That paid for my transportation to college. Now I had to believe for a job at college to pay for my tuition and other needs. Upon arrival, I applied for scholarships and grants, but I still desperately needed a job. I applied for a position to be a dishwasher in the college cafeteria. However, they told me that thirty people had applied for the job before me and that they would be hired ahead of me. I was very disappointed.

After applying, I went to the cafeteria for lunch. While I was eating my meal, the manager of the cafeteria came to my table. He asked if my name was Kevin, and I replied yes. He then told me that if I would go with him and begin washing dishes without delay, he would hire me ahead of the thirty people who preceded me on the list. I left my food on the table, followed him to the work area, and started washing dishes with a big smile on my face. I had a job!

Later I received grants from the government for some of my expenses. After that, I increased my credit hours per semester. Of course, this also increased my school bill. I was praying about that when I ran into a professor in the physical education locker room. I had favor with him because I had beaten the school record in two athletic events. He asked me if I needed anything. I replied that he could believe with me for my college tuition to be paid. He answered, "Oh, that's easy. I don't need to pray about that. I'll take care of it."

The next day, I received a call from the financial office, telling me that I had received another grant. Therefore, I decided to take classes during the summer as well, so my costs went up again. My bill skyrocketed so much that the university warned me that I would have to sit out a semester or two until the debt was paid.

After receiving that warning, I was at a friend's house, who had a beautiful painting of Jesus on the wall. While pointing at the portrait of Jesus, I told Him that I had left everything for Him and knew He wanted to pay off my school bills. It seemed like so much money at the time, but I knew He wanted to do it for me. When I spoke those words aloud, I knew they were correct and that I was merely voicing the truth. It is not enough to know something is true. You have to speak it out in words because your words release God's will on the earth.

A few weeks after this incident, I got a call from the registrar's office, asking me to visit them. I was well aware that the purpose of this appointment could be to ask me to leave college until I paid my bill. However, when I arrived the registrar handed me a copy of my school bill with "paid in full" written on it. As I sat there listening to the story of how that had happened, it became apparent that Jesus had performed a miracle for me.

The university's financial department was deeply touched by what God had done on my behalf. The registrar told me that a businessman had contacted them, looking for a student with an unusual last name. God had brought my face before the businessman, as well as my name, during prayer and told him to pay off my school bills.

He called all the universities in the city, asking for a student with my last name (which he didn't know how to pronounce) until he finally found my college. The man did not have a clear understanding of why he was doing this; he was just obedient to God. The man drove over to my campus and wrote a check for the full amount of my debt, but he requested that I never be told his name.

I want you, the reader, to be encouraged by this story of how quickly our heavenly Father can move on your behalf. If you will ask Him to help you, He will hear your cry from Heaven and come in a supernatural way to deliver you.

Chapter 5

GIVING TO THOSE WHO CANNOT REPAY YOU

IN A STUDY OF *SUPERNATURAL FINANCES,* ONE MUST CONSIDER a unique situation that will probably occur. There are certain circumstances where God has to come into the situation because the people involved sometimes just do not have the ability to repay the giver. A person who is the giver must recognize that he or she is responsible to move Heaven to receive payment for that which he or she has freely given. Often, the only recourse for the one who is the giver is to believe, in faith, that Heaven will repay him or her because the people who have received a blessing are in a situation where they truly cannot repay anyone.

ETERNAL REWARDS

While on earth, Jesus talked about eternal rewards at length. The Bible also discusses the topic of those rewards. The scriptures in this section concerning eternal rewards will minister to those who read them. The topic of eternal rewards is something that generally is neglected during a discussion about supernatural finances. Jesus did speak about a Christian's giving. Jesus emphasized this point—when one gives to those in need, it is best to do the act in secret. The expression that best fits this situation is perhaps the saying: "One hand does not even know what the other hand is doing." In the Book of Luke, Jesus says this concerning giving:

> So, now, go and sell what you have and give to those in need, making deposits in your account in heaven, an account that will never be taken from you. Your gifts will become a secure and unfailing treasure, deposited in heaven forever. Where you deposit your treasure, that is where your thoughts will turn to—and your heart will long to be there also (Luke 12:33-34 TPT).

When Christians give to those who cannot pay back, Jesus makes this fact clear—eternal treasure will be laid up for the giver. Christians who give must not expect a repayment from the one to who has received the gift. Christians also must not expect recognition for having helped another who is unable to repay. A perfect example of this type of situation is found in the story that Jesus told about the widow who gave her last two mites in the temple. Jesus and His disciples were standing in the temple near the spot where offerings were deposited. He was observing everyone as they gave offerings.

There were people who gave great amounts, and there were some who gave far less. And then there was the widow, who gave everything that she possessed. Supernaturally, Jesus knew that she had given all that she could give. She gave her total supply. There would have been no natural way to know that she had given her last two mites. Therefore, supernatural insight from the Father came to Jesus into the situation. But the key factor to consider is this one: Jesus saw her action, and He knew that this was all the substance that that widow possessed. When Jesus observed this widow and her gift, He turned to His disciples. He told them that what she had given was all that she possessed. Jesus said that she gave more than anyone else.

When that widow gave, she created a situation where she was dependent upon the Lord to come through for her in a miraculous way. She was not giving to receive the attention of people as others there were doing. She was giving because she wanted to give to God. Despite seeing that the widow gave all that she possessed, Jesus did not seek her out to give her money. He did not take the two mites out of the container to give them back to her. He did nothing. In fact, the widow assumed that no one even noticed her giving. Jesus, however, noticed her gift in the offering. He turned to His disciples and told them what the widow had done.

Jesus did not tell anyone to give the widow money. He did not instruct Judas, who held the treasury bag, nor did He tell any of the disciples to repay her. She gave everything that she possessed into the offering. She had no assurance of provision other than her faith that God would take care of her. God saw the widow's heart, just as He sees every giver's heart. There may be no immediate gratification or response to a person's offering that he or she freely gives. Christians must give from the heart, knowing that this is what God desires for His children to do. A Christian must be willing to obey God in any kind of situation, even a situation that is uncomfortable, such as giving to someone who one knows has no ability to return the favor.

We can be certain the widow who gave the two mites received a reward. We know that God is always faithful to give a return to those who give. But Jesus did not immediately compensate her or protect her in any way. However, God no doubt made certain that she received her reward. It is the same with any Christian who gives. God knows when someone gives an offering, gives of his or her time, or gives anything that he or she may do that can be considered a gift to the Lord. There may not be compensation that comes immediately. Sometimes, it is important to remember that when someone gives to others, some of those people who receive that gift are unable to repay that blessing.

Anyone who does things to obtain favor with man has the wrong motive. If a person gives with the motive of recognition, then that recognition is the only reward that will happen. If a person's motive is incorrect, that individual forfeits any repayment from the Lord. When a person does something for another person in secret, especially if the recipient is unable to repay the giver, that action causes God to assume responsibility for the return. Anyone who lends to the poor actually lends that gift to the Lord, and the Lord pays great dividends. This principle of God repaying when someone lends to the poor is found in the Bible. Jesus desires that those who give have the understanding that those gifts are viewed in an eternal perspective. The giver will definitely receive credit into his or her account for the items that he or she has given to help others.

When someone gives something with the correct heart motivation, there will always be a reward, and it is placed in the giver's eternal account with God. When a person gives, his or her gifts are secure, and a deposit is made in Heaven that lasts forever. Anyone who gives must evaluate his or her heart to ensure that the motive for giving is right in the sight of the Lord. A giver also must not look for a certain way that God will reward that gift. The Lord will determine the manner in which He will reward the gift.

No Worries

[Jesus said,] *"I repeat it: Don't let worry enter your life. Live above the anxious cares about your personal needs. People everywhere seem to worry about making a living, but your heavenly Father knows your every need and will take care of you. Each and every day he will supply your needs as you seek his kingdom passionately, above all else. So don't ever be afraid, dearest friends! Your loving Father joyously gives you his kingdom realm with all its promises! So, now, go and sell what you have and give to those in need, making deposits in your account in heaven, an account that will never be taken from you. Your gifts will become a secure and unfailing treasure, deposited in heaven forever"* (Luke 12:29-33 TPT).

It is important not to spend time anxiously thinking about a difficult situation. Christians need to be led by the Spirit. A believer must determine, in his or her heart, the way to handle a situation. When a believer takes the time and effort to ensure that the planned actions are of the Lord and then follows through with those actions, that believer has made a statement in Heaven. God says that He is going to daily supply all of the needs of His own dear children. A person who seeks God's Kingdom passionately can expect God to give back generously. He is a rewarder of those who seek Him (see Heb. 11:6).

Our heavenly Father joyously gives His children the Kingdom with all its promises. Every Christian must have assurance that God takes note of every gift that a believer gives. It is best to give gifts to the Lord out of a heart of thankfulness. Believers must not seek to identify the avenue which God will use to return the gift.

Christians need not worry about life because God has a plan for each and every believer's life. It is important to remember not to allow worry to enter into your thoughts. Christians are to live above anxious cares about personal needs. God will supply all of the needs of His own.

> *And this same God who takes care of me will supply all your needs from his glorious riches, which have been given to us in Christ Jesus* (Philippians 4:19 NLT).

Every Christian must realize that our heavenly Father knows every need. Our loving Father joyously gives every believer His Kingdom with all of its precious promises. The scripture says that deposits are made in each believer's account in Heaven. It is an account that will never be taken away from a Christian. Every gift that a Christian gives is safe, secure, and unfailing. Those things which a Christian gives are a treasure deposited in Heaven forever.

HEAVENLY TRANSACTIONS

A Christian who gives to others in the physical realm is also giving to others and in the spiritual realm as well. In that manner provision is made for reward in the life to come. Everything that a believer gives in this realm is going to be laid up to his or her eternal account. A Christian is wise when he or she discovers ways to give so that no one can pay anything back except for God Himself. When giving out of a right heart, a believer causes heavenly realms to activate and moves the angels to start to minister. God's children are to be people who will do righteous acts without seeking recognition or repayment. It is best to not allow good deeds to be known publicly, but to do good deeds in secret.

Each Christian must allow God, as a heavenly Father, to reward him or her. God says that Christians must not do things for the admiration of others. In the New Living Translation, Matthew 6:1-4 states:

> *Watch out! Don't do your good deeds publicly, to be admired by others, for you will lose the reward from your Father in heaven. When you give to someone in need, don't do as the hypocrites do—blowing trumpets in the synagogues and streets to call attention to their acts of charity! I tell you the truth, they have received all the reward they will ever get. But when you give to someone in need, don't let your left hand know what your right hand is doing. Give your gifts in private, and your Father, who sees everything, will reward you.*

Every believer must know that one's motives have to be right, especially in giving to others. When a Christian gives a gift in private, that action motivates God, the Father, to reward that person on His own. The best way to give is to do so without expectation of return from those who receive. A believer should have expectation of a return from the loving Father. Jesus also spoke in parables concerning this particular truth concerning giving to those who could not compensate the giver.

> *Then Jesus turned to his host and said, "When you throw a banquet, don't just invite your friends,*

relatives, or rich neighbors—for it is likely they will return the favor. It is better to invite those who never get an invitation. Invite the poor to your banquet, along with the outcast, the handicapped, and the blind— those who could never repay you the favor. Then you will experience a great blessing in this life, and at the resurrection of the godly you will receive a full reward (Luke 14:12-14 TPT).

These are the very words of Jesus! He is saying that Christians should concentrate on giving to the people who cannot help themselves. When a Christian seeks to follow that advice, the Bible promises that the believer will experience a great blessing in this life, as well as a blessing at the resurrection when each believer will receive a full reward. God rewards Christians in this life, as well as in the life to come! That is a wonderful exchange!

HELP PEOPLE

One way to receive a blessing in this life from God is to give to people who cannot pay anyone back for that gift. Those who cannot repay include the handicapped, the blind, the outcast, and the poor. The Holy Spirit wants people to realize the importance of blessing those who need a blessing. At this time, people often wrongfully focus on using influence to help one to succeed in life. Even within the church, a corporate culture has developed that forgets the poor and those who are in need who cannot help themselves.

However, Jesus said that when a person helps people in need, he or she has done that very act to Him. He takes it personally. For example, when a believer takes the time and effort to visit people in jail, Jesus says that person visited Him! He also says that every

Christian must recognize that whatever he or she has done to the least of those here on earth, it has been done to Jesus.

It does seem, in this day and age, that many believers have forgotten the importance of ministering to the people who have great need. There is a sure reward when a Christian ministers to people who have nothing to give in return. The Lord said:

> *And then those on his left will say, "Lord, when did we see you hungry or thirsty and not give you food and something to drink? When did we see you homeless, or poorly clothed? When did we see you sick and not help you, or in prison and not visit you?" Then he will answer them, "Don't you know? When you refused to help one of the least important among these my little ones, my true brothers and sisters, you refused to help and honor me." And they will depart from his presence and go into eternal punishment. But the godly and beloved "sheep" will enter into eternal bliss* (Matthew 25:44-46 TPT).

Jesus said Christians are to minister to those around them, and that includes the poor and those who are in need. He wants Christians to prosper. One way to prosper in God's view is to help those in need who cannot pay anything back to the one who helps them. Christians are ministering as Jesus asks them to do when they minister to those people who have no ability to pay back anything for what they receive.

God is watching as believers have opportunity to give to those in need. When a believer does an action with a pure heart motive, Heaven takes note!

Jesus spoke from the heart when He discussed faith. He said when a Christian believes in their heart, and when they say the desire with their mouth, that very desire will come to fruition. A believer will have what he or she says. So, a believer can speak to a mountain and believe in their heart that the mountain will be removed. Then, what the believer says will definitely manifest and come to pass.

MATTERS OF THE HEART

Many people mistakenly believe that a person's mind is the deciding factor for determining to give freely. In a sense, the choice is determined by the mind, but the heart is the determining factor because from the heart come motives. One must determine to give with a pure heart motive. Therefore, giving to those in need to bless them actually is a heart thing. A person knows when he or she gives with a pure and holy heart motive. The sixth chapter of Hebrews reveals that God will reward those who diligently seek Him. It is very important to recognize that faith is of the heart. Faith is not of the mind. Giving with holiness originates in the heart, where motives begin. Faith is not something that originates in the mind. Yes, one must choose with the mind to give, but the heart is the factor that determines if the giving is something that has pure motive to act. With pure motives behind it, the giving of the gift will be acceptable in the sight of God.

Every Christian must realize that he or she must not allow himself or herself to be manipulated mentally when others try to convince that believer to give. God does not honor or respect the actions of anyone who tries to manipulate another to give. He does not accept such manipulations as righteous acts. God loves when a

Christian gives out of his or her heart freely, but He does not love it when people try to manipulate a believer to cause them to feel obligated to give.

God desires that each believer determine what they should give in their own heart. One example that illustrates how much God desires a Christian's giving to be sincere and not manipulated is told when Paul sent a message ahead to the Corinthians. He told the Corinthians that before he arrived they were to collect the offering. Collecting the gifts ahead of time, before Paul even arrived, would render any manipulation of people or any preying upon the emotions of people impossible. Paul also recommended that the Corinthians set aside a portion of their increase, and he stated that those who did set aside a portion not do that action out of compulsion. Paul emphasized the fact that God loves a cheerful giver! Giving is supposed to be a joyful action for the believer!

Giving should be something that a Christian wants to do.

FAITH IS OF THE HEART

If a Christian is doing something out of faith, then that person receives a reward. Also, if a Christian does something in the name of Jesus because they want to represent the Lord as a generous giver, then they will receive a reward. In 1992, when I had my first heavenly visitation, Jesus told me that there are two ways for a Christian to receive a reward. One way to receive a reward was giving to someone in the name of Jesus, even it was just a cold cup of water to somebody in need. A person will receive his or her reward according to Scripture. The other way to receive a reward is when a Christian is stirred in faith, and also in compassion, toward someone. The gifts a believer gives out of faith and compassion receive the Lord's reward as well.

Every believer must realize that without faith, it is impossible to please God. One must believe that God exists and that He is a rewarder of those who fervently seek Him (see Heb. 11:6). Therefore, a believer's actions must be born out of the faith, as well as be born of the heart.

Before any meeting where an offering might be collected, the best thing to do is to pray ahead of time before that meeting. One good strategy is to simply inquire of the Lord, "What am I going to be giving tonight?" Asking this question before attending a meeting helps ensure that a person will follow the Scriptures. It also helps circumvent any manipulation that may come from those in the meeting, through the offering message, or any other situation. A believer needs to take precautions so that he or she is not being manipulated into giving. In Corinthians, Paul spoke concerning preparation of the offering before a meeting took place. If a Christian will determine ahead of time what they will give, then they will feel comfortable with the gift that is given. They will already have heard from the Lord concerning the offering to give, and then the giving will be done in faith.

I follow this strategy. The Lord will speak to me concerning the offering. And then I ask my wife, "What is the Lord laying upon your heart to give?" Her response is almost always exactly the same figure that I have heard from the Lord. Almost one hundred percent of the time, the amount that I was led to give and the amount that my wife said we were to give are identical. Therefore, in that manner, the Lord confirms the amount that we are to give completely! And that confirmation gives us freedom and the opportunity to rejoice in our gifts!

A Christian is to enjoy giving, and not allow anyone to take that joy by making a gift compulsory. In other words, a believer must not allow the pressure from others to take the joy of giving from them by submitting to that pressure to give. The needs of the people will exist, no matter what happens. Christians must not fill a gap by throwing money, and they will know not to throw money when they seek God for the amount and refuse to give under pressure.

When Christians give offerings to the church, they are not wasting their investment or just throwing money around. Rather, in faith, they are placing their gift on the altar to God, and He is receiving it. Each institution or church that receives gifts must do so responsibly and must determine where that offering will go by seeking the Lord. But every Christian has a responsibility to find out what God is saying to give, as well as a responsibility to place that gift into the ministry where they feel comfortable in their faith. Christians must never give offerings when there is pressure to comply. One's purpose to give must not be a response to pressure, but rather a response to the Lord and an expression of love toward Him.

THE SUPERNATURAL ATTITUDE

It is important to emphasize that the attitude of a believer must be correct when giving to those who cannot pay back the gift. The correct attitude requires faith on the part of the giver. One must have faith to give in a way that does not reveal one's giving to others. When other people do not know that a Christian is giving, the giver must operate in faith to believe that a return will eventually come forth. A Christian's reliance upon God and his or her belief that He will reward the giving is actually an act of faith of that Christian. The reward will not arrive because a person knows that someone is giving. In contrast, the reward will arrive because the Lord knows what that person who has given a gift has done. The Lord will make certain that the giver receives a reward, so that reward requires a supernatural response. A believer must exercise his or her faith to believe that the reward will come. He or she must keep the giving anonymous. When a Christian becomes determined to help others at the point of their need, he or she must also realize that his or her angels, who are assigned to those Christians who give privately, are keeping track of everything.

Angels are fully aware when a Christian has given freely to those in need who are unable to repay the debt. The angels report that information to the Father and Jesus in the heavenly host's command center. Angels are careful to record a Christian's every action, and when a believer gives, all of Heaven becomes aware of that act of kindness. It takes great faith to give in secret. It takes great faith to give to someone who cannot pay the gift back. So even though a person may believe in the existence of God, he or she must also have confident assurance that He is a Rewarder of those who diligently seek Him.

The Holy Spirit will notify the angels when a believer has given freely and privately to those in need. When the angels hear this news, it becomes their responsibility to ensure that the giver receives compensation. The angels will be certain to notify God, and the Christian who has given freely will obtain favor beyond what he or she could ask, think, or believe. A believer must have confident faith, choosing not to worry that this process will work. At first, a believer can begin giving small gifts to those who cannot give back in return. Doing small acts of giving often will help build a Christian's level of faith to give to people who cannot pay back. If a believer will start giving in secret, he or she opens the way for the Lord to reward that act of giving. Believers now live in exciting times! This process is supernatural, and Christians can have assurance that God sees their giving and will reward them.

SUPERNATURAL HELP

At this present time, there is more angelic activity happening than has ever occurred in any time of history! The Book of Acts reveals information of events that happened over the process of many years, yet the Bible documents only a certain amount of angelic visitation during the time of Acts. Sometimes one angelic visitation recorded in the Book of Acts actually happened after twenty years passed from the time of another visitation! When Christians read about those visitations in Acts, they often mistakenly get the impression that they all occurred within a few months. However, in reality the visitations often were separated by many years.

At this present time in the history of the world, we are having more angelic activity than ever before now. Angelic activity is also continually increasing. People are being visited in in a greater way. We are approaching the end of this dispensation, and it is God's desire for His children to prosper. Therefore, especially at this time in history and this age, the Lord seeks to reward His own for those things they have done in secret. Due to the acceleration of angelic activity, believers will begin to see evidence of an increase in the supernatural realm.

Angels often surround us at this time, and they see every act of giving one may do, no matter how small that act may be. Christians can, therefore, have great assurance that those angels will report what they are doing in secret. A report will be recorded in Heaven. When a believer takes the time and effort to help someone who is unable to help themselves, angels will report that action to the Lord. For example, angels will be watching and recording seemingly small things, such as when a person helps someone who cannot walk well to cross the street, or helps someone by holding a door for them, or helps another person by paying for his or her lunch in secret.

RANDOM ACTS OF KINDNESS

Christians have many opportunities to do random acts of kindness in secret, and those are the types of things that God desires for believers to do. The acts that believers do to show kindness produce a witness of the goodness of the Lord. One reason that the Lord desires for His children to have supernatural finances is to provide a means for believers to help others. Obedience is very important to God. Jesus has instructed me personally, and at great length, concerning obedience. One factor that is of great importance to the Lord concerning obedience is this one: Christians must obey Him immediately.

One of the greatest ways that God has taught me obedience and to hear His voice has been through dealing with finances. It is challenging to give freely when one has worked hard to achieve financial success. When the Lord presents an opportunity for someone to give of his or her own resources, which he or she has worked to accumulate, it is a test of that person's faith.

In my own life, while walking with the Lord, I have begun to realize that He has greatly instructed me in the area of finances. He wanted to see if I would listen to His voice. God can speak to a person and teach that individual how to hear His voice. Often, the Lord will take the opportunity to speak to someone concerning obedience through dealing with finances. The enemy of our souls, the devil, is generally not going to tell anyone to give money away! I have found that if I have the impression that I am supposed to do something for someone, the chances are great that the impression originates in the Lord. It is God's great desire to help people. And while He prompts a person to help another, He probably is teaching the giver some important concepts at the same time. A Christian needs to be aware that the devil is not going to tell anyone to give good things to another person! Generally, if a believer is impressed to give a gift to another person, the source of that impression is the Lord!

GOD'S VOICE

There have been times in my life when I was impressed by a voice saying, "I want you to give everything you own away." Yet, I knew that the impression to give everything away was not the Lord speaking to me. It actually was a familiar spirit, an evil spirit, trying to influence me to do something that would not please the Lord. It is true that there are times when the enemy, the devil, does try to give a Christian an impression to give. Therefore, when a Christian receives an impression to give, he or she must be careful assess that leading to assure that it is not the enemy who is trying to confuse him or her. However, for the most part, a believer can be assured that the Lord is not asking him or her to give everything he or she possesses away all at one time. Most generally, the Lord will ask a believer to give and help people as He prospers that believer. The usual pattern for Christians to expect is that God will ask a Christian to help others in ways that produce larger increments at each new opportunity that the Christian is led to give. Those increments increase over time as God prospers the believer more and more.

I have given a great deal of money away, and I have sometimes given in very large amounts. There were times that I gave almost everything I owned. However, in each of those instances, I knew that my giving was fulfilling the prompting of the Lord to give so abundantly.

My main point, however, is that Christians should listen to the voice of the Lord and follow His promptings, which generally are to give small portions at first. The Lord may speak to a believer concerning donating time to other people when it seems that that believer does not have any time to spare. There are instances when a person's donation of his or her time is worth as much as giving money, especially if the person already has a very busy schedule. Time can be an expensive gift when someone has a very busy life!

There are several important questions that Christians must ask themselves concerning finances. They must ask, "What is it that I desire in my life?" A believer must also ask, "What is the Lord speaking specifically to me?" Additionally, "What am I asking of God?"

The Holy Spirit will help a Christian reach an ideal place in his or her financial well-being. If God were to reveal His plans concerning every believer, it would be clear that those plans are far greater than he or she could ever think, believe, or ask! It is important that Christians begin to recognize that they are not dreaming big enough for their lives. God has many extremely big plans for every one of His children.

Despite feeling restrictions financially that seem to limit the possibilities in this realm, a Christian must not allow the view of the limitations to restrict his or her spirit. A believer must permit God to allow him or her to think big and to dream big. Every believer must not allow feelings to place limitations upon what the Lord can do! A Christian must allow the Spirit of God to take him or her beyond the limitations of the mind. Then, they will be ready to receive those things that God has for them. The plans that God has for every believer are far better, and far greater, than anyone could possibly anticipate. Most Christians are just not believing in a big enough way. The Lord wants to do supernatural things for every Christian. His desire is that every Christian will have super-natural finances. However, in order for those supernatural finances to come forth, God will ask a Christian to do things that are far beyond his or her ability to finance. The Lord desires Christians who will walk with Him as they increase in faith. As believers walk with Him in this way, financial impartations are given to those who will dare to obey God and do that which seems impossible. With God, all things are possible, and in the area of giving God will train a person to trust Him to do those things that one couldn't believe were doable!

The financial realm of a Christian who is willing to move for-ward in faith and trust the Lord fully with his financial well-being will expand to accommodate those things that God has already spoken to that believer. Whatever it is that the Lord has ordained as a believer's mission in the financial realm will come forth when a believer follows God in faith, doing what God has prompted him or her to do.

One must ask oneself several questions during this time of training in financial issues: "What is it that God has spoken to me to do? Is what I am about to undertake actually big enough to meet God's expectations? Am I filtering out what the Lord is saying because I am placing limitations upon the situation that the Lord does not approve?"

Each individual must recognize that if the impression to give is coming from God, that amount may very well seem to be an impossibility! If the amount does appear to be impossible, then chances are the prompting to give that amount is of God. When a believer has assurance that the prompting is from the Lord, he or she must recognize that it is essential to immediately obey God's voice. A person can have great confidence to walk into such a situation because in times previously, he or she began to sow. That seed planted long ago has already begun to create provision for those things which a believer will face in future times of testing. The finances that a Christian has sown faithfully at a previous time will have created a fund for the future!

More than twenty or twenty-five years ago, my wife and I began sowing a harvest for the future. Now, we are encountering financial prosperity because the Lord is coming through with the harvest. We are experiencing financial prosperity at such a rate that it is at the level of one tsunami after another for us financially. Many years ago, the Lord entrusted us with smaller amounts of money. We often gave not just money, but we gave our time, even when it did not seem that we had time to give. We gave our time, doing what God had asked us to do. At this moment in our lives, we are finding that

God gives us more and trusts us more as we experience this wonderful life in Him!

In conclusion, whatever it is that God is saying to each individual, he or she must take the limits off of any expectations. A person must allow God to expand his or her dreams to the point that their giving goes far beyond what anyone would think was possible. God will make the impossible truly possible in the lives of those who will listen to Him, believe Him in faith, and obey Him!

Financing Your Dream

God will frame a Christian's dream or vision, and then fulfill that dream or vision by sending forth supernatural finances. Step by step, a Christian may realize that he or she is impressed to give to those who are unable to give anything in return. God prepares the way for the supernatural things of the Lord to occur to meet financial dreams. As the Lord leads a Christian into more and more giving, and He provides things supernaturally, He is unlocking that Christian from the world's system of finances. He moves that Christian into a realm where His spiritual system of finances in life begins to operate. In our particular situation, my wife and I found ourselves giving to people who were so poor that it seemed as if they would never be able to give us anything back.

However, although it appeared that those people would never be able to return the gift we had given them, many of those people are now very wealthy. The wealth that they obtained was a result of our investment in them. When we helped them, God actually worked through my wife and me to bless those whom He desired to bless. As a result of the investment being prompted by God in the past, now these same individuals are able to do for others what we did for them. They are investing in those people whom God impresses them to help. These recipients are people who seem to have no hope or possibility of ever giving any repayment. As a result, the ones to whom we gave help observed what we did. They turned to do the same type of giving to others as God prompted us to do, and a cycle of supernatural financial blessing began.

One of the reasons that Christians are upon the earth is to help one another. God desires that believers have financial wealth. What is not permissible is for wealth to have a hold upon a Christian! It is important to remember that angels are watching over Christians who are giving to those who have no possibility of returning the gift.

The Lord told me that I was to assemble three Thanksgiving meals with all the fixings and turkey and give them to my pastor at my church to hand out to three families who needed the supplies or they would not be able to have Thanksgiving. So, I did what the Lord had impressed upon me to do, and the pastor gave them to the three families on Thanksgiving. The church usually did this every year, but they could not afford it this particular year, so they were touched, as well as the people who received the meals. I got a call telling me that the meals were distributed and that it was a touching moment to the families as well as to the staff at the church. I became overcome with the goodness of God. I hung up, and then the phone rang again. I had spent seventy-five dollars in total for the three meals. Not even thirty seconds had gone by, so when the phone rang again I thought it was the pastor. I thought he had forgotten to tell me something and was calling me back. It was a family member who was notifying us that we were inheriting seventy-five thousand dollars. They needed our information so they could transfer the money.

Jesus has taught me that there are things that we can do that will cause Heaven to have to act on behalf of others who cannot pay us back. He showed me that if we do things for children, the angels that are with them, who always see the face of their Father in Heaven, will go and tell on me. Then I will be significantly rewarded for doing these things for a child. He also said that when you take care of the widow and the orphan, your actions cause Heaven to be required to act on your behalf when you feed the poor. God will have to repay you. He also showed me that when you do not deliver yourself in a situation, then Heaven is required to deliver you, and your next step will be a supernatural step.

Angels are watching when Christians do things in secret.

I know that the power of the Lord is present as I write this information, and I am just going to pray over you and impart to you what the Lord desires for you to have from Heaven:

> *I pray, in the name of Jesus, that you would get a glimpse of what is happening in the spirit realm that surrounds you right now. There are angels all around you at this very moment. I tell you, by the Spirit of God, that I see angels standing by you now, and they are right beside you. They have been assigned to you. The angels are believing that you are going to grasp what you have just*

read, and that you are going to start to do things for people who cannot pay you back. You are going to start to determine in your heart that you can give far more than you ever thought possible without feeling guilty about giving more than it seems that you can give. I break that spirit that is coming against you that tries to manipulate you to give. The Lord is asking you to give only what is set in your heart, not out of compulsion, and not out of pressure. His desire is that you give out of a heart that is thankful. When you find that sweet spot where you can give out of thankfulness, the joy of the Lord is going to be made full in your life. And I break the powers of any familiar spirits that are presently manipulating anyone into giving in an area where the Lord is not leading. The Lord is going to speak to you in a powerful way, and you are going to know exactly what you are supposed to do. You are being set free right now! I break every witchcraft spirit, every manipulative spirit, and every familiar spirit. Those spirits that the enemy uses must cease, in the name of Jesus! The Lord says you are doing well. He says, "You have actually given more than what I even expected, and I appreciate it." This is what the Lord is saying to you right now! Rest in peace, and know that God is watching over your finances, and His ways with your finances are supernatural. Amen!

Chapter 6

THE GOD OF FAVOR AND COVENANT

IN THIS CHAPTER ON SUPERNATURAL FINANCES, I WANT TO share with you about God's favor. As we talk about the favor that God brings, we want to focus on scriptures that will bring you into fresh revelation on His favor. Favor is hard to explain because it's literally when God decides that He is going to do more than we deserve or can even handle! The favor of God is similar to the glory of God in that it's not easily definable. Favor is even hard to explain by some who have experienced it. It remains a mystery to most people.

Did you know that God is allowed to favor someone without consulting with anyone? Sometimes favor just occurs, and there is no logical explanation for it. At any moment, it is possible to literally feel light and encounter the power of God. You can begin to encounter the glory of God in your own life through a visitation and walk away with the favor of God as a result. It can happen as quick as reading this. It's time that you start seeing the favor of God more often in your own life. We must have the faith that believes that the power of God is ready to bring us into the culmination of the knowledge and wisdom of God to influence our lives in a significant way.

THE FAVOR CHECKLIST

God Looks!

> I will look on you with favor and make you fruitful and increase your numbers, and I will keep my covenant with you (Leviticus 26:9 NIV).

The idea in this passage is that the Lord looks toward us and His face shines upon us with a smile. When the Creator looks our way, He can cause favor to overcome His children. They become fruitful and, in that fruitfulness, it increases their numbers. God will always keep His covenant with you. In other words, the agreement that a person has with God is what He is going to honor. Everyone who serves God is going to benefit from His power and dominion.

Rely on His knowledge and wisdom. There is nothing we can do about the situation once He decides that He wants to bless us. Favor and goodness are going to overcome you!

His Face Shall Shine

> And the Lord spoke to Moses, saying: "Speak to Aaron and his sons, saying, 'This is the way you shall bless the children of Israel. Say to them: "The Lord bless you and keep you; the Lord make His face shine upon you, and be gracious to you; the Lord lift up His countenance

upon you, and give you peace."' So they shall put My
name on the children of Israel, and I will bless them"
(Numbers 6:22-27).

There are many references in this passage that are very powerful, specifically about God's countenance. His face is the grace and
shining glory emanating from Him. You need to understand this
awesome truth that, right now, God is noticing you. He is looking and smiling upon you and there are rays that come out of His
face that are going to touch your life in a tremendous way. His glory
is going to reroute your life. God will begin to take notice of you,
smile, and act on your behalf!

We have entered into the place that is called the favor of God.
The result of financial freedom is that supernatural finances have
come and are accomplishing the will of God. It may be unexplain-
able as God maintains the flow of finances from Heaven. A person
who experiences this is not "working God" and convincing Him to
show favor. He is the One who is working His overcoming power
toward those who commune with Him because He is *"The Lord
your God who loves you!"*

Turning the Curse into a Blessing

Because they hired against you Balaam the son of
Beor from Pethor of Mesopotamia, to curse you.
Nevertheless the Lord your God would not listen to
Balaam, but the Lord your God turned the curse into
a blessing for you, because the Lord your God loves you
(Deuteronomy 23:4-5).

Here we have the story about Balaam. Though the evil prophet
Balaam was going to curse Israel, God would not allow it because

God loved His people. He loved them so He turned the curse into a blessing. Whatever it is that we are going through right now, even if people are cursing us or we feel like there is a curse over us, know that when God has favor on a person, He loves them and looks upon them to turn it around. As children of God, we are going to see amazing things happen in our lives because God has chosen to take those curses and turn them into blessings. Curses do not hit us the way the enemy intended because God has crowned us with favor. Always remember that our heavenly Father has crowned us with glory and honor because He made us in His image according to Genesis 1:26. Because we are in His image, we can turn and look at Him face to face. We can behold Him and know that He has ordained us to walk with Him. We are fearfully and wonderfully made like Him, and He has ordained us to prosper and to live in blessing every day!

Surrounded by Favor

> But let all those rejoice who put their trust in You; let them ever shout for joy, because You defend them; let those also who love Your name be joyful in You. For You, O Lord will bless the righteous; with favor, You will surround him as with a shield (Psalm 5:11-12).

The Lord will bless the righteous with favor. The Almighty will surround us as a shield of protection. In faith, we must trust in Him. He is going to defend us. We are going to shout for joy because Jesus has the victory. Those who love Him are going to be joyful. He blesses the righteous with favor.

Crowned with Glory and Honor

> When I consider Your heavens, the work of Your fingers, the moon, and the stars, which You have ordained,

*what is a man that You are mindful of him, and the
son of man that You visit him? For You have made him
a little lower than the angels, and You have crowned
him with glory and honor* (Psalm 8:3-5).

In these passages we read of the created works of God that we
can enjoy by what we see with our natural eyes. We must also realize that God has visited us spiritually. God is great and yet He has
honored and recognized us. Favor comes when God does all these
beautiful things because He wants to visit and interact with us. He
wants to be part of our lives! Our heavenly Father wants to impart
the favor that has been given to Jesus on His throne in Heaven. He
wants to transfer this to our lives on this earth so each of us can
walk in favor. He has literally crowned you with favor.

He has crowned us with glory and honor because He made us
in His image according to Genesis 1:26. He created us in His image
so we can turn and look face to face. We can behold Him and know
that He has ordained us to walk with Him as a friend.

Enduring Favor

*For His anger is but for a moment, His favor is for life;
weeping may endure for a night, but joy comes in the
morning* (Psalm 30:5).

Favor is for life. God, through covenant, makes it permanent.
God has decided to favor us through Jesus Christ, and that favor is
now permanently on our lives. Even though a person might be weeping now, it is going to turn to joy because God is coming through
for us very shortly. Be encouraged because the Holy Spirit is willing to walk us into financial freedom. The ways of God have been
revealed through the Word of God. Once we have yielded to His

ways and acted on His desires, He is going to show up and help us. It will be beyond what we have ever asked or thought. Supernatural finances are the ways God has chosen for His children.

God Delights In Us

> By this I know that You favor and delight in me because my enemy does not triumph over me (Psalm 41:11 AMPC).

In other words, there is a victory that's guaranteed when we stay close to the Lord because the Lord is a warrior Himself. Even Zephaniah 3:17 (NIV) He is the "Mighty Warrior who saves." He is a Victor; He does not lose a battle. Whenever we are with Him, then we know that we have the favor that He carries.

Delight in Jesus who has triumphed over all. Hell knows that they are our enemies and cannot triumph over us because God is with us through His Son, Jesus Christ.

Because of Favor

> For they did not gain possession of the land by their own sword, nor did their own arm save them; but it was Your right hand, Your arm, and the light of Your countenance because You favored them (Psalm 44:3).

God's right arm and the light of His countenance are strong and powerful enough to rescue us. God Himself will help us because He favors us. We should be rehearsing this verse in our spirit all the time. Meditate on the fact that God has chosen to deliver His own. He has chosen to be our strong right hand and has caused our countenance to ignite. God is smiling on you!

Time of Favor

> *You will arise and have mercy on Zion; for the time to favor her, yes, the set time, has come* (Psalm 102:13).

Yes, the set time has come through Jesus Christ. We do not have to wait. Favor in our finances is here. God has chosen to come into our situations and help us. Favor is in your house and your life right now! Right now, begin to acknowledge that extraordinary changes in your life are imminent and that help is on the way because He has chosen to favor you.

Obtaining Favor

> *A good man obtains favor from the Lord, but a man of wicked intentions He will condemn* (Proverbs 12:2).

What does it mean to be good? The true meaning of goodness comes from the very throne of God. It is the very Person of Father God Himself. If we are believers, then we shall be the very imitators of God.

Webster's 1828 Dictionary defines good as follows:

1. Valid; legally firm; not weak or defective; having strength adequate to its support; as a good title; a good deed; a good claim.

2. Valid; sound; not weak, false or fallacious; as a good argument.

3. Complete or sufficiently perfect in its kind; having the physical qualities best adapted to its design and use; opposed to bad, imperfect, corrupted, impaired. We say, good timber, good cloth, a good soil, a good color.

And God saw everything that he had made, and, behold, it was very good (Genesis 1:31 KJV).

4. Having moral qualities best adapted to its design and use, or the qualities which God's law requires; virtuous; pious; religious; applied to persons, and opposed to bad, vicious, wicked, evil.

As a believer, continue to associate with the One who is good and walk with Him genuinely every day.

Therefore be imitators of God [copy Him and follow His example], as well-beloved children [imitate their father] (Ephesians 5:1 AMPC).

The Upright Have Favor

Fools mock at sin, but among the upright there is favor (Proverbs 14:9).

Those who chose to walk upright or straight on the path of life have favor from God. Fools do not have discretion and laugh at the correct path. A believer who trusts in God and His favor will experience supernatural finances in their lives.

Marriage Brings Favor

He who finds a wife finds a good thing, and obtains favor from the Lord (Proverbs 18:22).

A Christian who desires a spouse can hold on to this scripture and believe for a godly mate. Even someone who has an unbelieving spouse and wants to believe concerning that spouse's salvation can use this scripture because God can change hearts. The believer will obtain favor in the situation as well. God can redeem those who have not accepted salvation by the believing spouse. Continue to pray for the unbelieving mate and tell the Lord that favor is coming into the person's life.

The Heavenly Father's Honor

If anyone serves Me, let him follow Me; and where I am, there My servant will be also. If anyone serves Me, him My Father will honor (John 12:26).

Serving God will bring honor into our lives. Jesus encouraged us to follow Him with all of our heart. Following Jesus is key to having favor manifest, including finances. The word honor is defined as follows in *Webster's 1828 Dictionary*:

1. The esteem due or paid to worth; high estimation.

A prophet is not without honor except in his own country (Matthew 13:57).

2. A testimony of esteem; any expression of respect or of high estimation by words or actions; as the honors of war; military honors; funeral honors; civil honors.

3. Dignity; exalted rank or place; distinction.

I have also given thee that which thou hast not asked, both riches, and honour (1 Kings 3:13 KJV).

Thou art clothed with honour and majesty (Psalm 104:1 KJV).

4. Reverence; veneration; or any act by which reverence and submission are expressed, as worship paid to the Supreme Being.

5. Reputation; good name; as, his honor is unsullied.

6. True nobleness of mind; magnanimity; dignified respect for character, springing from probity, principle or moral rectitude; a distinguishing trait in the character of good men.

In doing a good thing, there is both honor and pleasure. When you follow God you obtain favor and God will be with you in a mighty way.

Working Together for Good

And we know that all things work together for good to those who love God, to those who are the called according to His purpose (Romans 8:28).

In this declaration made by the apostle Paul, he communicates the idea that if a person loves God, Heaven is going to work everything out so that it is in their favor. The Lord of favor will cause a person in financial distress, even if they have lost money or had it stolen, to rely on this scripture in Romans—that God is working it all out together for their good. Always remember that our loving heavenly Father has our best interests at heart. In favor, God is going to overcome every situation on your behalf. All we need to do is continually declare and reiterate this promise and it will break the devil's power.

God Is for Us

> *What then shall we say to these things? If God is for us, who can be against us? He who did not spare His own Son, but delivered Him up for us all, how shall He not with Him also freely give us all things?* (Romans 8:31-32)

Through the precious promises of the covenant, we have received everything we need for life and godliness (see 2 Pet. 1:3). Through Jesus, the favor on us will not allow disappointment to come in because God is for us and no one can be against us. We will always win! You always have the advantage because God is with you. He has delivered you up and is continually causing you to obtain victory as He has freely given you all things.

The Righteousness of God

> *For He made Him who knew no sin to be sin for us, that we might become the righteousness of God in Him* (2 Corinthians 5:21).

Jesus Christ has wholly cleansed our past and given us a position of acceptance before Father God. Rest knowing that this is so! All our past sins have been wiped away as a believer in Jesus and all things have become new; we are new creatures in Christ!

Adoption as Sons

> *But when the fullness of the time had come, God sent forth His Son, born of a woman, born under the law, to redeem those who were under the law, that we might receive the adoption as sons* (Galatians 4:4-5).

We obtain favor because God comes into our situation where we are orphaned, and He lovingly adopts us and brings us to His house. Father God has taken us out of the bondage. This is the perfect situation; we have been adopted into the family of God, and as a result we receive everything our heavenly Father has for us. We have inherited it because we were adopted in Him and so we must understand that favor comes through adoption. We are no longer orphans left alone. God came and signed the adoption papers and brought you into His family through Jesus Christ, and because of that favor comes into your life.

Because God has redeemed and adopted us, we are now sons and daughters of God. We have all rights, privileges, and benefits that God has given His children.

Accepted in the Beloved

> To the praise of the glory of His grace, by which He made us accepted in the Beloved (Ephesians 1:6).

Jesus has made us accepted through His blood. Here Paul is telling the Ephesians salvation is complete in God. He has worked it all out and done all that is necessary for the adoption. As a believer, we are in the family of God.

We are absolutely accepted. As believers in Jesus, we are free from rejection. We need to break the spirit of rejection, which also includes poverty, in our lives. We have financial freedom through Jesus Christ. There is a spirit of rejection and poverty in the world's system toward the church. It makes it seem like a committed Christian does not fit in. The apostle Paul told the Corinthian church to stand out and be separate from the world (see 2 Cor. 6:17). It's time to not be conformed to this world but transformed. A true believer in Jesus is not going to fit into the world's system any more than Jesus Himself fits in.

The reason we do not fit in is that the world system is wrong and full of corruption. We have the right system in the Kingdom of God. We are going to feel rejection when we are dealing with the world. That system has a king called lucifer, the god of this world. God has not accepted it. That is why Cain killed Abel. The whole thing that happened there with those two brothers represents satan's influence in the fallen world. Cain was of that system of satan (the world) and Abel represents the system of God or the Kingdom of God. Cain did not master lucifer and his system that was attacking him. Because of the spirit of poverty and rejection attacking Cain's mind as a result of the fall, he ended up killing his brother Abel.

We see the same situation being played out in this day that we live in. The world system and the people of the world cannot resist this worldly system because it is the spirit of the evil one. Satan, the god of this world, the prince of the power the air has taken over the world system. Unbelieving people in the world cannot resist the power of darkness. If we are born again by the Spirit of God and have the Holy Spirit living within, we can come against lucifer and his evil kingdom with the Word of God and the name and blood of Jesus. Start driving out devils and break the power of the enemy. Help the family, the church, by properly engaging the enemy. Let us start to build our local church and believers everywhere.

What occurs when a believer becomes spiritually influential in their territory? What happens is that we encounter dominance as individuals and eventually as a group of people called the Ecclesia or the church. In the original Greek language, it is the *Ecclesia*, known as the "called out ones," believers, and separated ones. Once you get a group of people who are called out from the world, then not only are you accepted in the beloved, you are rejected by the world. It's because you have a group of people who stick together and can deal with the warfare of being *in the world* but not *of the world*. Being part of the *Ecclesia* is essential to breaking the poverty and rejection that is consistently being promoted by the world system against believers, the *Ecclesia*.

We are the Church of the Living God, the Body of Christ. By the power of God, believers gather together and are not rejected because we gather among those who are the believing ones. We all need to find a place where we can be with people who have like faith. We can find believers who can come into agreement and can edify one another. Let us gather and edify each other and show that we are accepted.

God has accepted us by the blood. However, we need to realize that we are called out to be separate from the world. The world cannot be a friend. The world will never be our friend because they have an evil ruler named lucifer. We are spiritual people as believers, and the unredeemed cannot handle spiritual people. They do not have any way to talk to or communicate with a believer on a spiritual level because they are in deception. Therefore, you need to find others who are of like faith and dwell and spend time with them. Encourage each other and then you will overcome rejection because it is from the world rejecting you because they are of a fallen system with a fallen people. And those people in that fallen system will not inherit the Kingdom of God.

Everything Counts

I want to discuss another insight that Jesus gave me that can help you accomplish all He has planned for you. He wants you to fulfill every word that is written about you in your book (see Ps. 139:16). Some truths might be hard to accept at first, but they are necessary for success. First, everything we do in obedience to His Word counts in Heaven. Also, everything we do in His name—even things that seem insignificant, like giving a sandwich to someone—will not go unrewarded (see Mark 9:41).

Nothing is insignificant to the Lord. We are to be obedient to everything He tells us in His Word and by the Holy Spirit speaking to our hearts.

After graduating from college in 1985, I attended a two-year program to prepare for the ministry. However, upon graduation from this program, the Lord led me to seek employment with Southwest Airlines. A vision in 1986 showed that Southwest would hire me in two years. Two years later, in the exact month that I had the vision, I was in fact employed. During the first five years of my employment with the airline, I fed the homeless and talked to people about Jesus in many cities where I spent the night.

In the second week of December in 1999, I was in Burbank, California and did my usual thing, which was to leave the hotel after check-in to get something to eat. During my return to the hotel, I walked through a busy commercial area and ran across a homeless person, who was turned away from me and covered in blankets. This person, who I thought might be a woman, had the usual shopping cart overflowing with belongings. I had no food to give, so I asked the Lord silently what I should do. I heard the Lord say, "Give her twenty dollars." I obeyed, but reluctantly, because I was saving money for my wife's Christmas present and I never gave cash to homeless people, for obvious reasons.

When I approached her, I was not prepared for what happened next. I spoke loudly to get her attention and when she turned to me, I handed her the money. I could not see her face because of the blankets draped over her head. When she pulled the blankets back, I saw she had bright blue eyes and appeared to be a woman.

I told her that God loved her and that He wanted her to have this money. She quickly responded, "You have done what the Lord has asked you to do, and I was sent to warn you that hard times are coming to America. God wants you to prepare and be careful with every dollar and to use them wisely." When she finished speaking, she handed me back my money. Stunned by the message and the messenger, I wondered who she was because homeless people do not prophesy or return twenty-dollar bills, especially during the Christmas season.

Having turned to walk away, I thought, "I'll ask her name." Less than two seconds had passed before I turned back to find that she was gone; even her cart had disappeared. She had been only two feet away! I looked in every direction. In a matter of seconds, she would have had to travel a hundred feet to disappear from view.

Because of that angelic word, I took my money out of the stock market. Within five months of the visitation, the market began to crash and wildly fluctuate, but my money was safe. After the market dip of September 11, 2001, I was delighted that the angel had warned me because my losses were minimal. By February of 2002, I had fully reinvested. The funds in which I reinvested had fallen between 60 percent and 80 percent before I got back into the market. I rode the funds up as the markets improved until July of 2008. Unknown to me, this was the top of the market and I would soon receive another warning.

THE SMALL THINGS

While seated with my wife in the Seattle airport, I had another visitation. This time I felt as if someone came to stand by me as the Holy Spirit surrounded me. Then the word of the Lord came, saying, "It's time to get out. The markets are going to crash again." That was July 2008, and I had sensed something was wrong with the economy. Now I knew it was time to act. I responded immediately and got online with my laptop, and within ten minutes I had cashed out of my investments.

By the end of September 2008, the markets were falling again, but I did not lose a penny. The following spring, I reinvested into the funds that I had previously owned. They had still lost between 60 and 80 percent. The market returned to higher levels by 2013, and I successfully rode the market back up for the second time.

Because of the heavenly warnings, for the past nine years, I have been in the market only during the upturns and not during the downturns. I now have over four times my original investment because of the angelic warnings. Obviously, this would be impossible without Heaven's help. However, it doesn't end there; I have had more financial warnings that I will discuss in future books.

I was curious why the Lord told me about the two major market crashes and a third one that is to come but did not disclose them to the professionals involved in the economy. I don't know of anyone who predicted both the 2001 and 2008 market crashes. So, I decided to return to Burbank, California to thank the Lord for what He had done for me.

I went to the spot where the angel had appeared as a street person. Holding the printout of my retirement portfolio, I stood in a moment of silence on that spot. I thanked God for quadrupling my investments and asked why He had been so gracious to me. In the silence, I heard these words clearly: "I kept track of every sandwich you gave to a poor person, and I was just paying you back." Night after night for five years, I did that for Him, and He remembered that small thing.

Take care of His business, and He will take care of yours—everything counts!

PRAYER

I break the power of every evil spirit harassing you. I break the power of poverty over your life. I speak against every evil spirit that's hindering you. I break debt! I break fear in the name of Jesus! I break rejection in the name of Jesus, and I command every evil spirit to leave now in the name of Jesus! I break every deceiving spirit! Any evil spirit that is trying to keep revelation from flowing from everybody reading this book, I break your power in Jesus's name! I drive you out! I command you never to come back!

Let God's people go now. In Jesus's name, you are forever set free. I thank You, Lord, by the Spirit of the Lord. Right now, Holy Spirit, just open the eyes of every person to see that You have supernatural ways of dealing with people and their finances and that You are acting in their lives right now setting them free. A spirit of breakthrough is coming. I thank You, Lord, that You are overturning every situation and causing the enemy to flee. You are set free by the name of Jesus.

Thank You, Lord, for words that will come at night in dreams and visions. You will coach and talk to Your people and tell them how. Show the people how to get out of the situations they are in. Satan has tried to bind them up in those chains, but they are broken right now in the name of Jesus. I thank You, Lord, for setting Your people free. I thank You for the power of the Spirit that baptizes people in the Holy Spirit and fire right now. Thank You, Lord, that they pray in the Spirit, continually praying without ceasing in the Spirit. Give them a revelation in the name of Jesus concerning financial freedom.

Lord, I thank You for supernatural finances for Your children in the name of Jesus. Amen.

Chapter 7

THE ALMIGHTY'S WORD

It is the same with my word. I send it out, and it always produces fruit. It will accomplish all I want it to, and it will prosper everywhere I send it (Isaiah 55:11 NLT).

NO ONE IN ALL CREATION CAN COMPARE TO THE LORD GOD Almighty. He always was, He always is, and He is always to come. The apostle John wrote, "Each of these living beings had six wings, and their wings were covered all over with eyes, inside and out. Day after day and night after night they keep on saying, 'Holy, holy, holy is the Lord God, the Almighty—the one who always was, who is, and who is still to come'" (Rev. 4:8 NLT). The Lord surely has established His will for each one of His children's lives. He has good plans for His sons and daughters. Therefore, every Christian must seek Him with all their heart to know the great plans that God has for their lives.

Remember that in God's great power and existence, He also loved His creation enough to send His own Son to die in the place of anyone who will accept His offer of salvation (see John 3:16). No Christian should ever doubt the love that the heavenly Father has for each of His own. Even before we were ever born, God wrote about each one of us in His book (see Ps. 139). Therefore, His plans for us are perfect and wonderful!

THE ESTABLISHMENT OF HIS WORD

In the Book of Psalms, the Lord reveals that His plans are firmly and completely established. "But the Lord's plans stand firm forever; his intentions can never be shaken" (Ps. 33:11 NLT). We must never forget that we are His children, His very own sons and daughters. Therefore, God's plans for us are unshakable! We need to grasp these truths of God and believe that He has a place for each of one us within the beautiful plan and purpose that He has ordained. Always remind yourself of these truths.

We must also realize that the Lord's plans for us are eternal. His plans will continue for each of us forever, as long as we choose to allow those plans to come forth. When we walk closely with Him, staying in step with the Holy Spirit, we can be assured that we will continually live in the will of God and not stray from the path of truth. "Therefore, [there is] now no condemnation (no adjudging guilty of wrong) for those who are in Christ Jesus, who live [and] walk not after the dictates of the flesh, but after the dictates of the Spirit" (Rom. 8:1 AMPC).

Do you realize that whatever God has determined in His heart to accomplish for you is exactly what He will accomplish in your life? When we look to the Lord for help and He answers, God demonstrates that He has fully determined in His heart to fulfill the desires your heart. In other words, the desires of your heart will manifest because God says they will! Once the word is spoken, God will always establish His word.

It is essential to recognize that God's throne is the ultimate seat of power for all creation. He has thoroughly established His throne and will always have a foundation that will not be shaken. Therefore, each one of us can have the confident assurance that once God has spoken from His seat of power, those words are established as a foundation of His rule forever. It is crucial to remember that God's words are eternal and everlasting.

God's plans and intentions for us concerning supernatural provision are firmly established. Remember, God always desires to see His Word come to pass. The prophet Jeremiah says, "For I am alert and active, watching over My word to perform it" (Jer. 1:12 AMPC). This means that if we are able to determine what God has spoken concerning a particular area of our lives, then we can be assured that we are partnering with God in that particular truth. Supernatural provision is one of those awesome truths spoken by God. Supernatural provision is absolutely provided for every believer who will dare to take God at His word. Throughout the Bible, the Lord has demonstrated and confirmed repeatedly that supernatural provision is one of His basic truths for all those who will simply believe.

Through His Word, the Lord has spoken things over His people that are very powerful and easy to comprehend. We already know from the prophet Jeremiah that our heavenly Father has plans for each of His own children to prosper (see Jer. 29:11). In the life of every believer, the Lord is continually looking over His Word. Whatever it is that the Lord has spoken, He is fully aware and cognizant of what He has said. And He *always* remains true to His Word. He is constantly watching over His words to make sure that what He has promised will come to pass in your life.

As believers, our responsibility to His Word is to implement faith in what God has promised. Never forget that faith is what releases His promises into our lives! Implementing faith is essential to supernatural provision in our lives. When we exercise our faith, the actions corresponding to that faith will arise. Blessings will literally overtake us when we choose to activate our faith. Faith makes it possible for God to accomplish all that He intends for us. Faith makes it possible for each one of us to receive what God desires to pour out on our lives. We must always believe God for everything! We must continually remind ourselves that nothing is impossible to those who believe (see Mark 9:23). Standing on God's promises is always a key to receiving His blessings.

Because the Lord is watching over His Word concerning supernatural provision, we must learn to become a good receiver of blessings from His hand of grace. He has lovingly provided much prosperity for us. In His generous hand, the Lord has great prosperity for each of His sons and daughters. He is going to pour out tremendous blessings upon the life of everyone who will receive those blessings by faith. It is our responsibility to be willing and ready to receive the tremendous blessing that God desires to pour into the lives of His own.

IT IS TIME TO BE FULLY CONVINCED

The Lord through the prophet Isaiah clarifies any doubt that may be present concerning the longevity of God's Word. God and His Word will never be diminished by time. We must be fully convinced that God is able to outlast anything or anyone. Everything natural will fade away, but God Himself will endure forever. Every word that God speaks is a spiritual word that is an everlasting word.

What God says is permanent. What God says will be in effect forever. We must keep those things close to our hearts that the Lord has spoken to us concerning supernatural provision. It is essential to recognize that whatever God has said to each of His children is also something that He has already said in His written Word. The prophet Malachi said, "For I am the Lord, I do not change" (Mal. 3:6).

Because the Lord is everlasting, whatever He says is also everlasting. God's words do not change because He is everlasting and full of truth. The Lord has not changed concerning what He has written about you, nor does He ever change concerning what He has spoken over you. God's truth is permanent. It is exceedingly important for each us to trust God, especially in the area of supernatural provision. Jesus is consistently faithful. He does not change. "Jesus Christ is the same yesterday, today, and forever" (Heb. 13:8).

Three important truths to remember about Jesus concerning *supernatural finances* in the life of every Christian are:

1. Jesus is the Preexistent One. He existed before any of us were ever born. Therefore, this financial system was in place long before His children entered eternity.

2. When He came to this earth, He came as the Son of Man. Jesus came so that by His life and His Word, He could show every believer how to live an abundant life. Jesus not only taught everyone

how to live, but He also taught in the areas of giving and receiving.

3. Before time began, He was the Son of God slain from the foundation of the world (see Rev. 13:8). Nothing catches the Lord by surprise! Therefore, it can be said that nothing concerning the finances of any child of God surprises our loving heavenly Father.

GOD'S TRUTH IS ABSOLUTE TRUTH

The Lord is known for proclaiming truth. He is not a man that He should lie, so everything He says is not only true but it also will, most assuredly, come to pass. The Lord's throne is based on *absolute truth*. Psalm 89:14 says, "Righteousness and justice are the foundation of your throne. Unfailing love and truth walk before you as attendants" (NLT).

It is essential to recognize that anything and everything that the Lord speaks is in the realm of truth. Therefore, anything and everything that the Lord speaks is forever binding. In other words, God always means what He says and says what He means. One may ask, "What does the Holy Spirit say concerning truth that is *absolute?*" Jesus testified an important factor concerning absolute truth. He spoke of the coming of the Holy Spirit on the day of Pentecost. He said that the Holy Spirit would be called the Spirit of Truth.

> *And I will ask the Father and he will give you another Savior, the Holy Spirit of Truth, who will be to you a friend just like me—and he will never leave you. The world won't receive him because they can't see him or*

know him. But you will know him intimately, because
he will make his home in you and will live inside you
(John 14:16 TPT).

Therefore, the Holy Spirit can be known as "Truth." In the same manner that justice and righteousness are the foundation of God's throne, truth is found within the Holy Spirit. It is correct to say that the Holy Spirit is Truth. According to Psalm 89, truth is found to be walking around the throne of the Lord as attendants. In the Book of John, Jesus discusses the ministry of the Holy Spirit. He clearly reveals that the Holy Spirit is not only the Spirit of Truth, but that He will lead and guide anyone who yields to Him in truth.

And I will send you the Divine Encourager from the
very presence of my Father. He will come to you, the
Spirit of Truth, emanating from the Father, and he
will speak to you about me. And you will tell everyone
the truth about me, for you have walked with me from
the start (John 15:26-27 TPT).

When the Holy Spirit speaks to any believer, He is speaking the Truth. The Holy Spirit is speaking from the realms of God toward that individual. God has, for each of His own children, good plans with an expected end (see Jer. 29:11 KJV). God not only says that He has good plans, but He will accomplish those good plans. He will manifest those plans in the physical realm. Jesus further explains the ministry of the Holy Spirit in the Book of John. He says, "However, when He, the Spirit of truth, has come, He will guide you into all truth; for He will not speak on His own authority, but whatever He hears He will speak; and He will tell you things to come" (John 16:13).

Believers can confidently know that the Holy Spirit will only speak the truth. Concerning the Holy Spirit's mission, Jesus states that the Holy Spirit will not only speak the truth, but that truth comes through Him from our heavenly Father. Therefore, the loving heavenly Father is speaking by His Spirit to us concerning every aspect of our lives. Knowing this, it is through the Holy Spirit that our heavenly Father speaks to us about provision and finances.

Father cares deeply about each one of us. He cares for mankind more than anything else in all of creation. God, through His loving and tender care, will provide for each of His own children supernaturally. He lives by this truth: He is a loving heavenly Father who cannot deny His own children, and that means He will not deny prosperity to us.

Jesus also said that the Holy Spirit would tell us of things to come. During my heavenly visitation in 1992, Jesus spoke concerning His revelation of things to come—the future for all believers. He told me that the Spirit would lead me into all truth, and that this leading would certainly include my finances.

It is essential to understand the truth. Truth originates in the throne room of the Lord. Each one will know truth through the Holy Spirit, as well as through the Word of God. When we know the truth, that truth becomes a crucial and integral part of our daily lives.

REVELATION THROUGH GOD'S SPIRIT

The apostle Paul said, "'Eye has not seen, nor ear heard, nor have entered into the heart of man the things which *God has prepared for those who love Him.*' But God *has revealed* them to us through His

Spirit. For the Spirit searches all things, yes, the deep things of God" (1 Cor. 2:9-10).

Each of us needs to learn to establish a deep trust in our heavenly Father's love for us. We must also establish a deep trust in the Lord's ability to accomplish all that concerns our lives. We must have revelation concerning this truth in order to advance and become successful in every area of our lives. One of God's greatest desires is that every Christian have a life that is successful. He desires that we succeed in everything we do for His Kingdom.

The Spirit says we must know the deep things of God. Knowing those deep things is essential for each one of us. Concerning the deep things of the Spirit of God, we must be ready to receive the revelation that belongs to us. The Lord has prepared special plans for those who love Him. Father God has chosen the Spirit of God to give us amazing revelations! Those revelations of the Spirit pertain to things concerning the heart of the Father.

The Lord, by His Spirit, is saying to you, "I love you with an everlasting love. I, long ago, thought of you and breathed you into your mother's womb. I wrote a book about your days before one day came to pass! You are in My arms and you are in My plans. I will see to it that all My plans for you come to pass. If only you will trust in Me!" (See Psalm 139:16.)

UNVEILING THE OTHER REALM

In the spirit realm, the Lord is looking at the future of our lives as if that future is His now! Therefore, we must not worry or have any concern about our future. Our Father has planned something far better for each of His children than anyone could ever plan for themselves. There are things that are planned for every one of us that the angels know but are hidden from us for the moment. I am amazed at the intricacy of God's ways and how wonderful His thoughts are toward us. The psalmist wrote, "How precious also are Your thoughts to me, O God! How great is the sum of them! If I should count them, they would be more in number than the sand; when I awake, I am still with You" (Ps. 139:17-18).

The Lord has an all-consuming desire to unveil truth in our lives. Keeping that truth in mind, each of us must consider what we desire in life. The Lord has a great desire to place us on a path to financial freedom. There is a blueprint in Heaven for every believer, and included in those plans is the blueprint for our financial future. That blueprint is far brighter than anyone could possibly conceive! There are angels that are assigned to help us, so it is essential that we ask God to open our eyes to the angelic realm. We must also ask God to open our awareness to all of the many benefits that are in Christ. Pray the prayer that the apostle Paul prayed for the Ephesians:

> *I pray that the light of God will illuminate the eyes of your imagination, flooding you with light, until you experience the full revelation of the hope of his calling— that is, the wealth of God's glorious inheritances that he finds in us, his holy ones!* (Ephesians 1:18 TPT)

The Word of Truth

Jesus continually reminded His hearers that the words that He spoke were the same words that His Father was telling Him to speak. He would remind everyone that His words are Spirit and are life. Jesus was taking the heart of His Father from the spirit realm and making it known in the physical realm. Jesus was able to make His Father known in the physical realm in three distinct ways. First, He made His Father known by speaking the very words of His Father.

Second, He made His Father known by all His actions, which were inspired by the words of the Father. And third, He made His Father known by healing humanity.

Manifestation of the truth is very important when one speaks about truth. In fact, believers must not just believe! We must speak what we believe. The words we speak activate angels. When we speak the truth, we are simultaneously agreeing with the words that are being spoken in Heaven. The power of God's truth resides in the spoken word. When we speak forth in agreement with the promises of God, it sets the truth of God into action!

Remember that angels are here to implement the will of God. Here are some important things to remember concerning that process:

1. The angels that are assigned to us will implement our words when they are spoken by the Spirit of God.

2. God speaks those words forth because He is the Spirit of Truth.

3. Manifestation of the truth will come.

4. Angels are on duty at this very moment to make manifest the Word of God and cause the truth to come forth into every believer's life.

5. The Son of God speaks, and we are set free!

Free Indeed

*Then Jesus said to those Jews who believed Him, "If you abide in **My word**, you are My disciples indeed. And you shall know the **truth**, and the **truth** shall make you* *free." They answered Him, "We are Abraham's descendants, and have never been in bondage to anyone. How can You say, 'You will be made free'?" Jesus answered them, "Most assuredly, I say to you, whoever commits sin is a slave of sin. And a slave does not abide in the house forever, but a son abides forever. Therefore if the Son makes you free, you shall be free indeed"* (John 8:31-36).

When the Lord comes into a person's life, He brings freedom with Him into that individual's life. At the same time, Jesus will also begin to free every believer in the area of their finances. God's provision in our lives carries a supernatural freedom. Therefore, satan's control and any power that he may have had over that person is completely cancelled. Satan has come to kill, steal, and destroy; Jesus brings abundant life (see John 10:10). Always remember this important truth that is in operation: the enemy of our souls, satan, no longer has the ability to influence a believer's financial life because God has placed supernatural authority in that person's financial realm.

The truth is ignited right now, as the Word of the Lord forms inside of each believer who receives this word. The truth will create a fire in each believer who will receive this word. Each person must speak the truth of the Lord Jesus from that fire that is stirring within us. Then, we must prepare ourselves to watch what will happen. The angels will begin to minister for everyone who takes God at His word. At the very hour that a believer speaks the truth of the Lord Jesus, the angels will move to bring solutions in the financial realm.

The Holy Spirit is speaking to each believer concerning the fire of God. Every Christian who will believe can have supernatural freedom in the Holy Spirit through the holy fire of God. Supernatural finances are on the way when any believer begins to yield to that fire. When we choose to believe the word, we will come out as purified gold when we emerge on the other side of that supernatural fire. As each of us pass our testing, we will see a reward in the hand of Jesus. God's desire and plan is financial success for every believer because He loves His children dearly and wants His children to prosper and be in health.

A MARITAL VISITATION

One evening during the first week of January in 1993, I was on my way home from church after music practice in Phoenix, Arizona, when my car filled with a strong presence of Heaven. It was as though someone straight from Heaven were sitting in the passenger's seat beside me. Then I heard what seemed to be an audible voice say, "You are going to Seattle this weekend, and you are going to meet your wife." I had never been to Seattle and did not know anyone who lived there. The visitation in my car ended when I arrived at the house where I was staying.

The lady I was house-sitting for was at home when I arrived and greeted me at the door. The presence of God was still on me, and she sensed that something supernatural had just happened to me. I told her that God had just spoken to me and I needed to pray. When we sat down to pray, the presence I felt while in my car showed up again, and we had a fantastic time of prayer. It was beautiful because Heaven came into that house and the glory rested on us. I then mentioned that God told me that I was going to Seattle and would meet my wife-to-be that weekend. She began to laugh and said, "I happen to be going to Seattle to visit someone this weekend, too, and I already know who your wife is. I have known her for a while. I believe she is the right one because every time I'm with her, I think of you. I will pick you up at the airport when you arrive and introduce you to several women at church on Sunday. However, I will not tell you who I think is to be your wife; I'll let God do that."

That weekend I flew up to Seattle. When I walked into the church on Sunday, my eyes immediately fell on Kathi, and I heard the Lord say, "There she is!" After service, I met her, along with a number of other single women who attended the church. Later my friend asked me which one was to be my wife. I told her that it was Kathi, and she said, "Yes, she is the one I had in mind for you." We laughed and pondered how this would unfold.

Later, in February, I returned to Seattle to ask Kathi for a date. On the fifth of February, we had our first date, and it was also our hour of visitation. The same presence that had come into my car and the house where I lived showed up again and stood by our table at the restaurant. We were immediately covered with the presence of Heaven. We sat there and wept, but we never took a bite of our food while God confirmed to each of us our future union. We had our meals boxed up and gave them to a street person on the way to the car. Eight days later, on the thirteenth of February, we were engaged; and on May 8 of that year, we were married in Selah, Washington, by four minister friends who believe in the supernatural.

Within just a couple of weeks, we got a phone call that surprised us. One of my wife's friends called her because she had found Kathi's name mentioned in a list of unclaimed property for the state of Washington. When my wife called, we received $10,000 miraculously from Jesus as a wedding present. The Lord is faithful. He can do many things like this to bless you as a surprise. He is good!

Chapter 8

UNDERSTANDING THE SACREDNESS OF THE TITHE

And all the tithe [tenth part] *of the land, whether of the seed of the land or of the fruit of the tree, is the Lord's. It is holy to the Lord* (Leviticus 27:30).

WHEN GOD CREATED THE HEAVENS AND THE EARTH, HE rested on the seventh day. He set apart that one day of the week, the seventh day, as holy. God gave the seventh day as a gift to mankind. Therefore, a person can give that special day as an offering to the Lord. The act of giving back the seventh day is one way that we can acknowledge the lordship of Jesus in our lives.

When the Lord made the Garden of Eden, He gave mankind access to everything except the tree of knowledge of good and evil. This tree was only for the Lord; it was not for mankind. All the rest of the garden was for man to use as he pleased. When the Lord does something for us, He asks for us to give a portion back to Him. God has a divine purpose with us providing a portion that we give back to Him; the purpose is that He desires that we acknowledge Him as the Source of the blessings.

Jesus was the fulfillment of the law. Therefore, Jesus did not abolish the law.

> *Don't misunderstand why I have come. I did not come to abolish the law of Moses or the writings of the prophets. No, I came to accomplish their purpose. I tell you the truth, until heaven and earth disappear, not even the smallest detail of God's law will disappear until its purpose is achieved. So if you ignore the least commandment and teach others to do the same, you will be called the least in the Kingdom of Heaven. But anyone who obeys God's laws and teaches them will be called great in the Kingdom of Heaven* (Matthew 5:17-19 NLT).

When I met Jesus face to face in 1992, I clearly understood that He was the solution to every problem that mankind has ever had. I should have known the fact that He is the solution to all problems more fully and more readily than I actually did. However, I did not fully comprehend it until I met with Jesus on the day that I died and was brought back to life. When I was with Him, I met Him without the limitations of this fallen world. I recognized more fully that Jesus is misrepresented and misunderstood here on earth more than any person who has ever walked the face of the planet. That Jesus is so misrepresented and misunderstood is an astounding revelation, especially when one considers He is actually the Creator of this planet!

Remember that from His preexistent state, He came to the earth in a body that was prepared for Him. "Therefore, when He came into the world, He said: 'Sacrifice and offering You did not desire, but a body You have prepared for Me'" (Heb. 10:5).

DO NOT MISUNDERSTAND WHY JESUS CAME

Jesus is the solution to every problem we have in this life. Our heavenly Father has sent His one and only Son into this world because He loves us (see John 3:16). Do not misunderstand why Jesus has come. The Father will help us in every area of life, including our financial health.

Jesus did not come to abolish the law of Moses, nor did He come to abolish the writings of the prophets. No, Jesus came to accomplish the purpose of the law and the writings of the prophets. He spoke truth when He said that until Heaven and earth disappear, not even the smallest detail of God's law will disappear. God's law will not disappear until the purpose of the law is completely fulfilled. The law includes what is written concerning us, as well as, every aspect of our lives. We are not to ignore even the least commandment.

Additionally, we must not teach others to ignore the least commandment. Those who ignore God's commandments will be called least in the Kingdom of Heaven. In contrast, anyone who obeys God's laws and teaches them everywhere will be called *great* in the Kingdom of Heaven.

The truth in the following passage should be part of the mindset of every believer. The truth in this scripture reveals the mindset that Jesus revealed. Jesus left everything in Heaven to purchase everyone who will accept the price that He paid. He created a way for every believer to have a relationship with our heavenly Father. This act was the most awesome and expensive transaction in history. Jesus was equal to God, and yet He willingly became a bondservant. At this very moment, Jesus is seated at the right hand of God the Father, interceding for His children.

> *Let this mind be in you which was also in Christ Jesus, who, being in the form of God, did not consider it robbery to be equal with God, but made Himself of no reputation, taking the form of a bondservant, and coming in the likeness of men. And being found in appearance as a man, He humbled Himself and became obedient to the point of death, even the death of the cross. Therefore God also has highly exalted Him and given Him the name which is above every name, that at the name of Jesus every knee should bow, of those in heaven, and of those on earth, and of those under the earth, and that every tongue should confess that Jesus Christ is Lord, to the glory of God the Father* (Philippians 2:5-11).

Jesus has not only redeemed us but has provided us with all of the benefits that belong to the children of God. We have abundance because of what Jesus has already done. In the context of finances and giving, the apostle Paul tells the Corinthians to continue to excel in their giving. "That in a great trial of affliction the abundance of their joy and their deep poverty abounded in the riches of their liberality" (2 Cor. 8:2).

Later in the chapter, Paul tells of Jesus Christ being the "Preexistent One" who left everything in glory in order for each of us to have it all. Paul, in the context, is talking about the giving of finances. Therefore, it is accurate to state that finances are part of our rich inheritance in Christ. "For you know the grace of our Lord Jesus Christ, that though He was rich, yet for your sakes He became poor, that you through His poverty might become rich" (2 Cor. 8:9). The Lord's salvation is great. God cares so much for His children. He is willing to do, for every single one of His own, far above what anyone could ask or even imagine. "Now to Him who is able to do exceedingly abundantly above all that we ask or think, according to the power that works in us" (Eph. 3:20).

A DEEPER LOOK INTO THE SACRED THINGS

The Lord instructs truth concerning the sacred things He must reveal. We must take the time to study and research deeply those sacred things of God. When a person attempts to study and know God's sacred things in depth, he or she can have a greater understanding to operate more fully in those things. Those sacred things are those things which God desires for His own. In Numbers 18, there are many profound truths revealed concerning special gifts, covenants, the tithe, holy offerings, and sacred things.

To understand these things in a fresh and deeper way, we must include two thoughts that are essential in understanding these ideas. That is, God's personality and the intent that He has for us. To understand these sacred things, I want to break the information into portions and discuss four distinct areas of these sacred things of God.

The Offerings Are Set Apart

> *However, you may not redeem the firstborn of cattle, sheep, or goats. They are holy and have been set apart for the Lord. Sprinkle their blood on the altar, and burn their fat as a special gift, a pleasing aroma to the Lord. The meat of these animals will be yours, just like the breast and right thigh that are presented by lifting them up as a special offering before the altar.* **Yes, I am giving you all these holy offerings that the people of Israel bring to the Lord. They are for you and your sons and daughters, to be eaten as your permanent share.** *This is an eternal and unbreakable covenant between the Lord and you, and it also applies to your descendants* (Numbers 18:17-19 NLT).

This is the first statement that God said concerning the sacred things—the firstborn of the livestock is set apart. God said, "They are holy and have been set apart for the Lord." It is clear that the Lord asks us to set apart, first of all, certain things in our life that He has given us. This is because He wants us to remember and worship Him as a Person and not the things He has given us. When we sacrifice the things that are sacred to Him, it is "a special gift, a pleasing aroma to the Lord."

Remember, God is in Heaven on His throne of power and authority. He loves to be worshiped by His creation. By making an altar and lifting up a sacrifice as a special offering before that altar, God is very pleased. The one who does these things will find favor with Him!

When a person receives anything that is precious to him or her, the first response that they should have is to worship God by lifting that gift up to Him in thanks. Everything a person may receive in compensation should be set apart to God. Even if God requires a person to give Him the best part, a person should offer it to Him with a thankful heart, knowing that the offering of that item will never be a loss. A person who worships God in this way will always triumph and cannot fail. There is an eternal and unbreakable covenant between the Lord and those who worship Him and honor Him with giving. This eternal, unbreakable covenant also applies to the descendants of those who will worship God and offer thanksgiving when they give offerings back to the Lord.

The Lord will even share His offerings with the priests (ministers) in the House of God. "Yes, I am giving you all these holy offerings that the people of Israel bring to the Lord. They are for you and your sons and daughters, to be eaten as your permanent share."

The Allotment and Tithe Are Set Apart

> *And the Lord said to Aaron, "You priests will receive no allotment of land or share of property among the people of Israel. I am your share and your allotment. As for the tribe of Levi, your relatives, I will compensate them for their service in the Tabernacle. Instead of an allotment of land, I will give them the tithes from the entire land of Israel"* (Numbers 18:20-21 NLT).

I like the statement that the Lord says to the priests through Aaron, *"I am your share and your allotment."* When we bring in the tithe to the local church or organization and present it to the Lord, we are providing for those leaders who minister to the Lord and to the congregation. The Lord considers those who minister to Him as His own personal assistants. Because these ministers are doing the work as the Lord directs them, they are to receive from Him personally. This is the share and compensation that God appoints to them.

Therefore, from the tithe that the people give, the Lord is able to care for those who minister to the Lord, thus providing a means for their living. Tithing is a holy thing due to two types of transactions. First, the transaction that happens between the giver and God causes tithing to be a holy thing. Second, the transaction that happens between God and His ministers causes tithing to be a holy thing. "As for the tribe of Levi, your relatives, I will *compensate* them for their service in the Tabernacle." God is willing and able to compensate the workers of His house because of the giving of the tithe, which is that which belongs to Him (Mal. 3:8-9).

The Lord determined and instituted the system of tithing, compensation, and allotment within His house. This system teaches God's children who are faithful to honor God as their source. Additionally, this system also honors those who are serving Him in His house. God actually gives the tithe to the workers of His house: "I will give them the tithes from the entire land of Israel."

The Levites and Priests Are Set Apart

From now on, no Israelites except priests or Levites may approach the Tabernacle. If they come too near, they will be judged guilty and will die. Only the Levites may serve at the Tabernacle, and they will be held responsible for any offenses against it. This is a permanent law for you, to be observed from generation to generation. The Levites will receive no allotment of land among the Israelites, because I have given them the Israelites' tithes, which have been presented as sacred offerings to the Lord. This will

be the Levites' share. *That is why I said they would receive no allotment of land among the Israelites* (Numbers 18:22-24 NLT).

Imagine how awesome it must have been to be one of the Levites whom God chose to be a part of serving and protecting the house of the Lord! Imagine hearing the statement from God saying that a Levite shall "receive no allotment of land among the Israelites, because I have given them the Israelites' tithes, which have been presented as sacred offerings" to God!

The Levites and the priests were to depend upon the Lord to receive their share of the tithe. The priests and the Levites were set apart from the rest of the nation of Israel unto the Lord Himself.

Actually, because of the work of Jesus, every Christian is similarly set apart to the Lord. We are set apart through revelation. He is the hope of glory within each of us and therefore He is continually available to every believer to be a Revealer of truth. As it says in Colossians 1:27, "Christ in you, the hope of glory." He helps us to understand important principles, especially principles that pertain to what we have through Him. "By having the eyes of your heart flooded with light, so that you can know and understand the hope to which He has called you, and how rich is His glorious inheritance in the saints (His set-apart ones)" (Eph. 1:18 AMPC). God desires that we become aware of those good things He has provided for every one of His children.

Because of sanctification through Jesus Christ, He qualifies us to receive the holy things of the Lord. When we begin to understand these principles of holiness, we will also begin to understand the state of ownership that belongs to every Christian. The Lord has freely given the state of ownership to all Christians. Each believer can become more and more aware of their ability to partic-ipate fully in supernatural finances within the Kingdom of God. As we walk in this knowledge of our ownership and act upon it, we become more fully aware of the part that ownership plays in supernatural finances.

A Sacred Offering

> The Lord also told Moses, "Give these instructions to the **Levites:** When you receive from the people of Israel the tithes I have assigned as your allotment, give a tenth of the tithes you receive—a tithe of the tithe—to the Lord as a sacred offering. The Lord will consider this offering to be your harvest offering, as though it were the first grain from your own threshing floor or wine from your own winepress. **You must present one-tenth of the tithe received from the Israelites as a sacred offering to the Lord.** This is the Lord's sacred portion, and you must present it to Aaron the priest. Be sure to give to the Lord the best portions of the gifts given to you" (Numbers 18:25-29 NLT).

The Lord gave these instructions to Moses concerning the Levites, the workers in the house of God. All the people of Israel gave that tithe. The Levites received that tithe. The Levites were even required to present a tithe of the tithe they received. They were to give their tithe to the Lord as a sacred offering. This was to honor the Lord and to acknowledge His provision for them in the house of the Lord. The workers of God's house were to demonstrate thank-fulness to Him through their act of giving tithes. The Lord knows the importance of thankfulness in establishing any relationship. A person is to give the Lord the very best portion of those gifts that He has freely bestowed upon us.

Those individuals who work in the house of the Lord are to be thankful for all that the Lord has done for them. They are not to treat the gifts of the Lord given to them by the people of the Lord as an ordinary thing. The Levites were considered to be holy and set apart. Therefore, the portion for them was part of the tithe received into the treasury of the house of God. The holy tithe was for the priests and the family to receive. It was theirs to meet all their needs as their livelihood.

I am so thankful that the Lord has compensation planned for those who serve Him. Even in the old covenant we can see God's heart for any person who gave their whole life over for service to the Lord. He gave those people a portion of the holy offerings. The principle that is revealed in the giving of tithes is that a holy God collects holy tithes and offerings from His people. He then gave that which is sacred to holy individuals, who were the Levites and priests, and who served in His house. Finally, God asked the servants of His house to additionally give a tithe of that allotment from the offerings they had received.

It is very important to recognize that all the truths about the tithe for the priests reveal God's heart for His supernatural Kingdom. Every believer's finances are supernatural. In the plan of God, the finances of every believer are part of an amazing Kingdom that is operating on the principles of Heaven. Believers are not to treat these gifts as common. They are to treat these gifts as holy and as sacred. If we will do the things God asks, we are not just separating ourselves from the world. We are also separating our finances from the world. Those who treat these gifts as holy and sacred will have proof that those gifts are holy and sacred. The evidence will come forth because God will most certainly begin to move supernaturally in the finances of those who acknowledge these gifts as sacred and holy. We must learn to trust God with finances and to not treat those assets as common things. God will turn everything around for a person supernaturally if they will place full trust in Him in the area of finances.

> *Also, give these instructions to the Levites: When you present the best part as your offering, it will be considered as though it came from your own threshing floor or winepress. You Levites and your families **may eat this food anywhere you wish**, for it is your compensation for serving in the Tabernacle. **You will not be considered guilty for accepting the Lord's tithes if you give the best portion to the priests.** But **be careful not to treat the holy gifts of the people of Israel as though they were common**. If you do, you will die* (Numbers 18:30-32 NLT).

WE ARE PRIESTS AND KINGS

The apostle Peter revealed very important truths concerning the priesthood that we must understand. Now that the finished work of Christ is accomplished, every child of God should fully comprehend that Jesus has made it possible for them to stand in the same situation as the priests and the Levites of the Old Testament. Believers are now the ones who offer up spiritual sacrifices to God. Because of the work of Jesus, we are now accepted as priests and Levites. There is no doubt concerning our position with Him. Jesus has accomplished His task of redeeming mankind. Because of His substitutionary role, everyone who accepts Christ as Lord has been placed in a position as a priest unto God. Jesus is now the high priest of our confession (see Heb. 3:1). Peter said, "Come and be his 'living stones' who are continually being assembled into a sanctuary for God. *For now you serve as holy priests, offering up spiritual sacrifices* that he readily accepts through Jesus Christ" (1 Pet. 2:5 TPT).

It is important for every believer to have the revelation of kingship. There are several powerful attributes that pertain to a king's ability to rule and have authority over his domain. When one is a king, his purpose is to rule and reign in power. Therefore, Christians are to demonstrate these distinguishing characteristics of ruling and reigning in power. Jesus essentially gave every believer the power of attorney to reign with Him in the heavenly realms. The apostle Paul, speaking to the Romans, said:

> *For if by the one man's offense death reigned through the one, much more those who receive abundance of grace and of the gift of righteousness will **reign in life** through the One, Jesus Christ* (Romans 5:17).

I want to reign in this life, and every single believer should also desire to reign in this life. No matter what we may encounter, we must endure to the end to experience victory. The Lord has freely provided everything necessary so that we can be successful in this life. You can move into financial freedom! This blessing will come forth as Jesus begins to deliver each believer who will trust Him financially. He will deliver that believer from the world system. They will move into the realm of a supernatural system of financial freedom that will cause great possibilities to be within their grasp!

The apostle Paul told Timothy, "If we endure hardship, *we will reign with him*. If we deny him, he will deny us" (2 Tim. 2:12 NLT). Every believer who wishes to be financially free must declare war against the enemy. However, we must also be willing to stand strong and persevere in the war, even during hardship.

In order to obtain freedom from this world's system, we must receive supernatural intervention. God will begin to interact with our finances as we begin to rule and reign with Him. Supernatural intervention will begin to create changes in our finances as we begin to think, say, and do as God desires concerning our finances.

True believers, those who are the church, are helping the Lord. We are His Body on the earth. God's purpose for His church is to defeat the enemy. Every member of the Body of Christ is essential to the victory that Christ wishes to bring for the church today. The apostle Paul says, "For Christ must reign until he humbles all his enemies beneath his feet" (1 Cor. 15:25 NLT). When we yield to the Spirit of God we become involved in the process of ruling and reigning. And we will be involved in ruling and reigning until all of the enemies of Christ are beneath the feet of those who belong to the Lord.

Even the eternal future of each believer in the millennial reign of Christ will reveal a priestly and kingly rule that they will obtain with Jesus in His Kingdom.

> *Wonderfully blessed and holy are those who share in the first resurrection! The second death holds no power over them, but they will be **priests** of God and of the Christ. And they will **reign as kings** with him a thousand years!* (Revelation 20:6 TPT)

Jesus Supported New Testament Tithing

One thing to remember concerning the tithe is the fact that tithing is not, as some people erroneously assume, strictly a principle of the Old Testament. Jesus explained this in the Gospel of Luke. He said:

> *What sorrow awaits you Pharisees! For you are careful to tithe even the tiniest income from your herb gardens, but you ignore justice and the love of God. **You should tithe, yes,** but do not neglect the more important things* (Luke 11:42 NLT).

As the overseer of the New Covenant, Jesus supported tithing. However, Jesus emphasized that justice and the love of God are greater than tithing. Jesus considered justice and love as "more important things." He did say that believers should still tithe, nonetheless. Christians should take heed of what the Master has spoken and not let tithing slip from their lifestyle. Christians are called to a supernatural lifestyle. Part of that supernatural lifestyle involves finances.

Abraham Tithed Before the Law

One interesting aspect concerning the tithe is the fact that Abraham knew that it was proper to tithe to the King of Salem, Melchizedek. Abraham tithed to Melchizedek before Moses was born. Therefore, Abraham tithed to Melchizedek before the Lord even gave Moses the law on Mt. Sinai. Moses, as you may recall, received detailed instructions concerning the tithe during his encounter with Jehovah on the mountain.

> *This Melchizedek was king of the city of Salem and also a priest of God Most High. When Abraham was returning home after winning a great battle against the kings, Melchizedek met him and blessed him. Then Abraham took a tenth of all he had captured in battle*

and gave it to Melchizedek. The name Melchizedek means "king of justice," and king of Salem means "king of peace." There is no record of his father or mother or any of his ancestors—no beginning or end to his life. He remains a priest forever, resembling the Son of God.

Consider then how great this Melchizedek was. Even Abraham, the great patriarch of Israel, recognized this by giving him a tenth of what he had taken in battle. Now the law of Moses required that the priests, who are descendants of Levi, must collect a tithe from the rest of the people of Israel, who are also descendants of Abraham. But Melchizedek, who was not a descendant of Levi, collected a tenth from Abraham. And Melchizedek placed a blessing upon Abraham, the one who had already received the promises of God. And without question, the person who has the power to give a blessing is greater than the one who is blessed.

The priests who collect tithes are men who die, so Melchizedek is greater than they are, because we are told that he lives on. In addition, we might even say that these Levites—the ones who collect the tithe—paid a tithe to Melchizedek when their ancestor Abraham paid a tithe to him. For although Levi was not born yet, the seed from which he came was in Abraham's body when Melchizedek collected the tithe from him (Hebrews 7:1-10 NLT).

Abraham knew that it was appropriate to tithe to Melchizedek. I believe that God Himself told Abraham to tithe to Melchizedek. The directive concerning tithing could have originated in a conversation that occurred during a visit between Abraham and the Lord. Abraham honored Jehovah with a tithe given to King Melchizedek, but not because of the law. Rather, he honored the Lord with the tithe because of his relationship with the Lord.

Our relationship with God should cause us to honor the Lord with the first fruits of our increase. When we bring the first fruits of our increase of substance to the God, we bring wealth into His house on earth. According to the prophet Malachi:

> *"Bring all the tithes into the storehouse, that there may be food in My house, and try [test] Me now in this,"* says the Lord of hosts, *"if I will not open for you the windows of heaven and pour out for you such blessing that there will not be room enough to receive it. And I will rebuke the devourer for your sakes, so that he will not destroy the fruit of your ground, nor shall the vine fail to bear fruit for you in the field,"* says the Lord of hosts; *"and all nations will call you blessed, for you will be a delightful land,"* says the Lord of hosts* (Malachi 3:10-12).

SUPERNATURAL TITHING BENEFITS CHECKLIST

1. Bring all the tithes into the storehouse.

The Lord has a designated a specific storehouse for each of His people to bring the holy tithe and present it to Him. Each of us must find out where that specific storehouse is located for our tithe. We can determine where that particular storehouse is located by guidance from our heavenly Father.

It is very important for every believer to have a local congregation that he or she calls home. Every believer needs a pastor who will spiritually look over and minister to them. A pastor is essential to help a Christian through tough times and to train them up in the ministry that God has for them. The local church where a believer is part of the congregation is the likely place where they should give the tithe.

Eventually, each believer has the opportunity to minister in the gifts that God has designated to them. We are given gifts so our capacity to minister in the local church can come forth. Being a blessing in a local church is part of God's plan and is one way to prosper in every area of your life.

2. Do this so that there may be food in My house.

God asks for the tithe to be brought into His house to provide for the needs of all who serve in the house of God. This provision is aligned with the instructions that God gave to Moses on the mountain. The purpose of the tithe was to provide for the needs of the priests and the Levites. The purpose of the tithe in the church today is to provide for the needs of the minister and the congregation.

3. Test Me now in this.

Malachi 3:10 says, "prove me now herewith" (KJV) concerning the bringing of the tithe into the storehouse. This verse is the only time in the Bible that God ever says that we are to test or try Him. One key phrase in Malachi 3:10 is worthy of note. God identifies Himself in this statement as the Lord of Angel armies or hosts. He reminds believers that He is the head over even the angels. The armies of Heaven are the ones who do God's bidding. They hearken unto His voice. The Lord Jesus has the power to command angels concerning every believer, and it is important for us to realize the power Jesus has to command His angels concerning us. God absolutely will take care of every believer who will trust Him and present the holy tithe to God's house. He will pour out blessing upon those obedient tithers with *supernatural finances*.

4. I will open for you the windows of Heaven.

The Lord not only possesses the keys to the windows of Heaven, but He also desires that His obedient children receive abundance of riches in glory from those open portals. If a Christian will tithe and obey God, according to these verses, they confidently expect a supernatural release of financial blessings upon their life!

5. The Lord will pour out for you such blessing that there will not be room enough to receive it.

The Lord wants to pour out upon His own such a blessing that they will not be able to find enough places to store the abundance. He desires that every one of His children receive everything that He will pour out upon them. The abundance of gifts that He desires to give is beyond what anyone could possibly imagine! We must be careful not to limit God with our own restricted vision, thoughts, or words. He will direct the paths of the righteous.

Each believer must give back a tenth of their substance to the Lord. When a believer trusts the Lord with the tithe, it removes restrictions upon God. The Lord is then free to perform the impossible in a believer's life. There is a guarantee that any who will be obedient in the tithe will not be able to contain the return, just as the Scripture says.

If tithing were not for today, the Word of God would not say that He will pour out a blessing that the recipient cannot contain. God desires to bless His children, and when they test His Word concerning tithing, He will, as He always does, prove Himself as true to His Word. Abundant blessings will pour out upon the tither. It is time for every believer to trust the Lord and tithe. In that way, God can show Himself true to His Word by pouring out an abundant harvest to His children.

6. I will rebuke the devourer.

> "I will rebuke the devourer for your sakes, so that he will not destroy the fruit of your ground, nor shall the vine fail to bear fruit for you in the field," says the Lord of hosts (Malachi 3:11).

The Lord Himself will rebuke the devourer for the sake of every believer who will take God at His promise to bless those who tithe. He will defend the borders of His own from all harm. The enemy will not be able to touch the tither's finances because those finances will have become supernaturally protected. Angels have been assigned to protect the substance of His tithers. The favor of the Lord will be upon His children's finances in a manner that will become quite evident to all.

7. All nations will call you blessed.

The blessings of the Lord will come upon those who will be obedient concerning the tithe. The blessing will be so evident that everyone around the tithing believer will know that God has moved upon that person's finances in a supernatural way. It is quite a thing to be blessed by God! However, when others begin to note that blessing, it is evidence of God's goodness. That evidence of the goodness of God in the blessing that He pours out to the tither brings the message of evangelism to the unbeliever! *Supernatural finances* can become the new normal in the life of every believer who will tithe and trust God at His promises. Then, a witness of the goodness of God to those who believe Him and are obedient to His ways will be made to those who do not yet know Him as Savior or as the One able to bless a person with abundance of substance. And that blessing will be far beyond one's wildest imaginations.

8. For you will be a delightful land.

Any believer who dares to put God to the test by tithing will eventually receive admiration from people who observe the life of that believer. People will also readily seek after those Christians who have put God to the test by tithing. When God is true to His promise to bless the tither, others will automatically admire them and seek after them because of the great delight caused by the blessing upon those obedient children.

> *And all the tithe of the land...is the Lord's. It is holy to the Lord* (Leviticus 27:30).

Remember to "Honor the Lord with your possessions, and with the first fruits of all your increase; so your barns will be filled with plenty, and your vats will overflow [Hebrew: burst open violently] with new wine" (Prov. 3:9-10). The Lord will not be able to ignore the one who tithes! He will send His angel armies to minister to every tither so that they will have more than plenty. God refuses to allow people to ridicule or make fun of Him without receiving consequences. A person will reap what they sow if they ridicule God or His children concerning the tithe. In Galatians, the apostle Paul says:

> *Do not be deceived and deluded and misled; God will not allow Himself to be sneered at (scorned, disdained, or mocked by mere pretensions or professions, or by*

His precepts being set aside.) [He inevitably deludes himself who attempts to delude God.] For whatever a man sows, that and that only is what he will reap (Galatians 6:7 AMPC).

The Holy Spirit says, concerning the promise in Proverbs 3:9-10, that if someone will honor the Lord with their possessions and the first fruits of all of the increase, it will guarantee that the barns of that obedient person will be filled with plenty and their vats will overflow with new wine. That scenario sounds as if it is pertaining to supernatural finances. And the truth is, it does pertain to supernatural finances!

THE SACREDNESS OF THE SABBATH

Remember the Sabbath (seventh) day to keep it holy (set apart, dedicated to God). Six days you shall labor and do all your work, but the seventh day is a Sabbath [a day of rest dedicated] to the Lord your God; on that day you shall not do any work, you or your son, or your daughter, or your male servant, or your female servant, or your livestock or the temporary resident (foreigner) who stays within your [city] gates. For in six days the Lord made the heavens and the earth, the sea and everything that is in them, and He rested (ceased) on the seventh day. That is why the Lord blessed the Sabbath day and made it holy [that is, set it apart for His purposes] (Exodus 20:8-11 AMP).

Jesus reveals the explanation for the true intent of giving back one day a week as an offering to the Father. That day was set apart as holy. Christians are to rest on the seventh day, just as God did during His week of creation. "Then Jesus said to them, 'The Sabbath was made to meet the needs of people, and not people to meet the requirements of the Sabbath. So the Son of Man is Lord, even over the Sabbath!'" (Mark 2:27-28 NLT).

Jesus is even Lord over the Sabbath. He taught His people to give the holy seventh day back to the Lord. Jesus permits us to do good things, even to the point of saving the lives of others. "Then he turned to his critics and asked, 'Does the law permit good deeds on the Sabbath, or is it a day for doing evil? Is this a day to save life or to destroy it?' But they wouldn't answer him" (Mark 3:4 NLT).

Every believer is to honor God with the first fruits of all the substance that they possess. Tithing is a way of honoring God for what He has given to His own. Every supernatural provision comes from Him, and it is essential to honor Him for that supernatural provision.

The Holy Spirit has given us direction concerning the sacredness of the Sabbath. Every believer should consider giving God a portion of their week. We should give that time as an offering to Him. Giving a portion of each week to the work of the Lord will cause the supernatural to flow into the rest of our work week. When we tithe our substance, effort, or time to the Lord, then God is willing and able to cause supernatural increase in our lives. He will cause that supernatural increase to come forth for every believer who dares to trust Him!

One morning, as my wife and I went down to the car from our apartment at the time, we realized that our car was not where we had parked it. Satan had stolen our car, so we immediately grabbed hands and prayed. We worshiped the Lord and thanked Him for getting our car returned to us in the name of Jesus. We were confident because we are people who practice tithing. We knew God would protect us. We also agreed that the people who stole the car would be caught as well and that we would receive full recompense.

Shortly after this agreement prayer, we called the police and filed a report. Because that particular type of car was rare, the police did not think that we would ever get it back. We did not agree with the police officer's assessment and began to pray. After approximately three weeks, we were contacted by the police department—they had found our car. A police officer on patrol in the early morning hours had noticed that our car seemed suspiciously backed into a 7-Eleven convenience store. When the officer approached the vehicle, the car alarm went off and locked the people in the car so that they could not escape or drive away. The police could not turn off the alarm even though the thieves had cut it. So, they disconnected the battery, which is the power source for the alarm. The car continued to go off the whole way to the impound area without any battery power. We got our car back, and the thieves had to pay restitution to us for the next three years. The car was cleaned and returned to us, so we got double payback for our trouble!

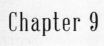
THE FEAR OF THE LORD AND GIVING

Therefore, having these promises, beloved, let us cleanse ourselves from all filthiness of the flesh and spirit, perfecting holiness in the fear of God (2 Corinthians 7:1).

GOD IS OUR SOURCE FOR EVERY GOOD THING. CHRISTIANS must realize that He is the source for our finances. He is Almighty God. He chose to pay a great price for everyone who will accept His plan of salvation. Therefore, Christians must reverence Him and fear Him. The Lord deserves the worship of His church because of the great things that He has done for every one of His children. In Second Corinthians, Paul emphasizes that Christians must not only cleanse themselves from all filthiness, but they must perfect holiness in the fear the Lord. When a person truly belongs to the Lord, then the possessions of that person also belong to the Lord. Christians have been set apart unto holiness.

The element of holiness concerns how a believer belongs to the Lord much more than how a believer may behave. In the heavenly Father's ownership, a Christian has become God's own private stock, His own private possession. The heavenly Father has made His children part of His own family. The Lord claims mankind as His own. He claims no other part of all creation as His own except for mankind.

Any Christian who desires to enter into supernatural financial blessing must first understand not only the true meaning of holiness, but also the fear the Lord. God is jealous over every one of His children; He wants them for Himself. The Lord desires that every one of His people become separate from the world. That means that His people must be set apart and holy. The separation unto holiness of each believer helps him or her to begin to walk more fully in the fear of the Lord. When a Christian walks in the fear the Lord, he or she moves into the beginning of wisdom and steps into the first phase of revelation.

In the early Church the phase of revelation began after the Holy Spirit was poured out upon the people. They began to move into the revelation of who they were in Christ. Because the early Church began to develop an understanding of their place in Christ, their lives influenced many people around them. The witness of the lives of the early Christians caused multitudes to enter into the Kingdom of God in a very short amount of time.

The New Testament testifies that multitudes received the word of God and were baptized in the Holy Spirit. Because people received the word and were filled with the Spirit, they began to move into the stage of revelation.

*And with many other words he testified and exhorted them, saying, "Be saved from this perverse generation." Then those who gladly received his word were baptized; and that day about three thousand souls were added to them. And they continued steadfastly in the apostles' doctrine and fellowship, in the breaking of bread, and in prayers. **Then fear came upon every soul, and many wonders and signs were done through the apostles** (Acts 2:40-43).*

God desires gifts that are set apart as holy. When a Christian presents a gift to the Lord, His expectation is that the gift is holy. A person's heart must be holy when he or she offers a gift to God. A Christian must prayerfully consider several factors when giving a gift to God. The giving of a gift to the Lord is a sacred activity, and therefore, the giving of a gift to God must be done with the correct motive, a clean heart, and a clear conscience.

If a Christian possesses the correct heart toward giving, he or she will have an awesome respect and fear concerning our heavenly Father. Each person who gives good gifts to the Lord must first repent of any evil ways and humble himself or herself under the mighty authority of the Holy One. Though God loves His own beyond what anyone could ever ask or think, He still requires holiness of His children. Therefore, Christians must be set apart from the ways of the world. When a person is joined to the evil ways of this earth, they do not have the quality or characteristic of holiness. Therefore, anyone who gives God a gift must realize that gifts cannot be attached to any ungodly heart issues. They must sincerely give gifts to the Lord that He is able to accept. He accepts gifts that are clean, pure, and holy.

In the Book of Acts, we read of an example of how God views giving with a heart that lacks holiness or with a motive that is not pure. A couple gave a gift to the church in Acts, but their gift was without holiness. They conspired together to be deceitful in their giving. There was no need for this couple to be deceitful. However, these two people had an unclean motive. Their desire was to be seen as givers in front of the people of the church. There was no need to lie about their gift, yet they lied, thereby truly deceiving only themselves, for God knows all things.

> *Now, a man named Ananias and his wife, Sapphira, likewise sold their farm.* **They conspired to secretly keep back for themselves a portion of the proceeds.** *So when Ananias brought the money to the apostles,* **it was only a portion of the entire sale.** *God revealed their secret to Peter, so he said to him, "Ananias, why did you let Satan fill your heart and make you think you could lie to the Holy Spirit?* **You only pretended to give it all, yet you hid back part of the proceeds** *from the sale of your property to keep for yourselves. Before you sold it, wasn't it yours to sell or to keep? And after you sold it,* **wasn't the money entirely at your disposal?** *How could you plot such a thing in your heart?* **You haven't lied to people; you've lied to God!"**
>
> **The moment Ananias heard those words, he fell over dead.** *Everyone was terrified when they heard what had happened. Some young men came in and removed the body and buried him. Three hours later, his wife came into the room, with no clue what had happened to her husband. Peter said to her, "Tell me,*

were the two of you paid this amount for the sale of your land?" Sapphira said, "Yes, that's how much it was."

Peter told her, **"Why have you agreed together to test the Spirit of the Lord?** *I hear the footsteps of those who buried your husband at the door—they're coming here to bury you too!" At that moment she dropped dead at Peter's feet. When the young men came in, she was already dead, so they carried her out and buried her next to her husband.* **The entire church was seized with a powerful sense of the fear of God, which came over all who heard what had happened** (Acts 5:1-11 TPT).

This story from the Book of Acts reveals how God views the motives of the heart in giving gifts to Him. This couple conspired to secretly keep back for themselves a portion of the proceeds. Their gift was only a portion of the entire sale, and they presented the gift as if it were all of the money from the sale. The apostle Peter confronted them both by the Holy Spirit. He said, "Ananias, why did you let Satan fill your heart and make you think you could lie to the Holy Spirit? You only pretended to give it all, yet you hid back part of the proceeds."

The apostle Peter was the authority in the church at that time. The Holy Spirit moved upon Peter to confront this couple concerning the motives of their hearts in the giving of this particular gift. Peter said that the money belonged to them entirely, but that they had plotted together to lie. The apostle said that they had not lied to the congregation, nor to the pastor. Peter stated the truth—their lie had been a lie to the Lord God. Those very words judged Ananias, and he fell dead when Peter spoke that truth. Later, when

Sapphira came in, Peter confronted her motives as well. Peter asked her, "Why have you agreed together to test the Spirit of the Lord?" When her response was also a lie, she fell dead in front of the entire congregation.

The church heard that these events had happened, and the entire body of believers was "seized with a powerful sense of the fear of God, which came over all who heard what had happened."

When giving gifts to God, the Holy Spirit wants Christians to fully consider the condition of the heart. When a Christian gives anything to God, he or she must possess respect and demonstrate reverential fear for the Lord. He or she must also give a gift with the right motivations and a demonstration of true holiness.

The Lord says that the fear of the Lord is effective in one's life. In Psalm 25:12-13 it says, "Who is the man that fears the Lord? Him shall He teach in the way He chooses. He himself shall dwell in prosperity, and his descendants shall inherit the earth." The fear of the Lord allows these amazing benefits to be manifested in a person's life:

1. The Lord will teach them in the way God chooses.

2. They will dwell in prosperity.

3. Their descendants will inherit the earth.

The Holy Spirit says powerful things to believers concerning the fear of the Lord. Those who do have the fear of the Lord will receive these good things—instruction, prosperity, and inheritance for their descendants. Understanding the fear of the Lord is the foundation of a Christian's financial health. Those who fear the Lord have a wonderful guarantee—they will lack no good thing. In Psalm 34:9-10 the psalmist says, "Oh, fear the Lord, you His saints!

There is no want [no lack] to those who fear Him. The young lions lack and suffer hunger; but those who seek the Lord shall not lack any good thing."

Christians, be prepared to receive what the Holy Spirit is saying. Those who fear the Lord suffer no lack. There is no lack for their descendants as well. A Christian who fears the Lord will ensure that the generations that follow him or her will be blessed, just as he or she has been blessed. Psalm 112:1-3 says:

> *Praise the Lord! Blessed is the man who fears the Lord* [worship and reverence], *who delights greatly in His commandments* [His Word]. *His descendants will be mighty on earth; the generation of the upright will be blessed. Wealth and riches will be in his house, and his righteousness endures forever.*

God blesses everyone who will fear the Lord. It is important to continue to worship Him. Anyone who fears the Lord will surely find that his or her descendants will be mighty on the earth. God's wealth will come to the house of those who fear God and worship Him in spirit and in truth. Righteousness will endure forever. Dare to fear the Lord, and be willing to move into supernatural finances and abundance as never before now!

I remember when Kathi and I first got married, we wanted a house so badly. The Lord miraculously gave us the ability to get a brand-new home built in Phoenix, Arizona. We both worked full time, tithed, and gave to others, and at the same time were able to meet our bills miraculously. However, because of the high electric bills to cool our house in the summertime in Phoenix, Arizona, it became costly to the point where we had to diligently look for quarters all over the house to get enough money together to pay our electric bill. We looked at each other and agreed that this was not God's will for us to make it, so we declared war on debt. Eventually, we got out of debt. God miraculously paid off the mortgage for our house. A family member had left us an inheritance to pay off our house. We were instantly out of debt in all areas of our lives. When our mortgage was miraculously paid off, it was right after the markets had crashed in 2008. A lot of people we knew at the time were having trouble paying their mortgage payment every month. We saw a supernatural miracle happen and everyone around us rejoiced with us because it was clear that only God could have done this. We stayed faithful in our tithes and offerings and believed that God saw that, and He got us out of debt. To this day, we pay our electric bill in advance for a whole year or two at a time to declare the victory to the devil who harassed us so much when we were a newly married couple. God enforces His covenant when we do our part, and it is exciting to be able to pay our electric bill two years in advance as a testimony to satan and the world.

> *The angel of the Lord stooped down to listen as I prayed, encircling me, empowering me, and showing me how to escape. He will do this for everyone who fears God* (Psalm 34:7 TPT).

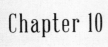

Chapter 10

A LESSON ON KINGDOM AUTHORITY AND DOMINION

And you shall remember the Lord your God, for it is He who gives you power to get wealth, that He may establish His covenant which He swore to your fathers, as it is this day (Deuteronomy 8:18).

TO LEARN ABOUT SUPERNATURAL FINANCES, IT IS IMPORTANT to understand the way that financial principles relate to the Kingdom of God and Kingdom authority. It is an exciting time now because the Lord is showing His children good things concerning finances and provision. Provision can be supernatural, especially in these last days. God shines a spotlight upon many areas of Christians' lives to direct them to a clear spiritual path for success. The Holy Spirit, through revelation, will shine into people's lives and help them know His truth about finances and provision. The truth of God sometimes does not just come to a person quickly. In this earthly realm, a Christian may have to fight for truth. However, truth will be revealed when a Christian persistently stands upon God's promises! Often, Christians must battle spiritually for a time until the outcome they desire manifests!

Momentum

There are evil spirits of darkness located here on the earth, and they are fighting against the truth. They are fighting against any Christian being able to understand the truth of God. Evil spirits are fighting against a Christian's destiny. Once a born-again believer receives the truth, those forces move into action to block that person from success.

For this reason, I was sent back to this present time so I can help people personally. I am here to teach Christians how to hold on to the promises of God until they are successful! We who teach the Word and who operate in the faith in the Word are here to break the power of the devil! We are here to teach other Christians how to increase the momentum for having victory in every battle that the enemy sends to stop them. God wants every one of His children to break free from the spirit of this world. If Christians will permit the Holy Spirit to reveal the things in life that are blind spots to their progress, then believers can have the triumph over the power of the enemy in life. The Lord wants all of His to children have victory in every area of life.

Kingdom authority is a very important topic that Christians must understand and learn to use. When a Christian begins to understand his authority in life, then victory in this life is certain to happen. This topic, Kingdom authority, is especially important to the lives of Christians today. The days in which we live are the last days before Jesus returns to the earth, and believers need to win the spiritual battles they face.

One may ask, "What is Kingdom authority?" In order to comprehend Kingdom authority, a person has to understand several things. A Christian needs to have an understanding of the King, His Kingdom, and His power. When God calls us believers (Christians), He gives us the authority to trample on serpents and scorpions. What Jesus said before He left the earth transferred His authority from the King and His Kingdom to the ambassadors, or the subjects, of the Kingdom. God's children are the ones who are ambassadors, or subjects, of the Kingdom of God. Christians represent Jesus Christ on this earth. Jesus is still fulfilling His ministry on earth. The Holy Spirit is on this planet to help Christians fulfill what Jesus began two thousand years ago. Through *believing ones*, God is able to cause the Kingdom business to happen in life. Christians must believe that He is our God, and that He is a rewarder of those who seek Him!

The Bible clearly states that *signs shall follow the believing ones.* Those signs shall follow Christians with supernatural finances. They are one of the most important things that a Christian can learn!

Christians need to develop an understanding of Kingdom authority, which is of major importance to each believer. A Christian who understands Kingdom authority has insight into areas that might have been blind spots without knowing about Kingdom authority. People may mentally agree that we have authority through the name of Jesus and in the blood of His sacrifice. They may have somewhat of an understanding that a believer walks in Kingdom authority. However, a successful believer must understand Kingdom authority from the perspective of the enemy of our souls. Satan is deceived and thinks that this world belongs only to him. He did steal the authority and dominion over this world from Adam and Eve, and he is aware of what the Lord has done for mankind. Through Jesus Christ, God has claimed His children back and redeemed them. One of the reasons that God purchased Christians through Jesus is so they can be ambassadors here on earth. The covenant, or agreement, that the Lord has created is between Himself and those on earth who have accepted Him as Savior.

DRIVE HIM OUT

Everywhere Christians go, they have a responsibility to drive the devil out! The devil is a liar, and he does not stand for righteousness, and he does not stand for absolute truth. Christian leaders must teach the Word of God correctly so that Christians can develop spiritually and become mature enough to defeat the enemy's continual strategy to deceive everyone. Most people do not want to be controversial; they just want to show love to other people, and that, in the right situation, is fine. However, when the devil arrives on the scene, Christians must be skillful in battle. They must be able to use the Word of God against the enemy. Satan does not respond to a soft, friendly tone. Christians must keep in mind that Jesus revealed that the devil is a murderer. Jesus said he was a murderer from the beginning, and therefore he does not have any good traits (see John 8:44).

While believers are on this earth, their thoughts, words, and actions should continually drive satan toward the lake of fire. Believers can constantly point our enemy in the direction of his eternal destiny. They must use the authority that God has placed within them to be effective in sending satan in the direction that he should be going, which is toward eternal separation from God and His sons and daughters.

We cannot be gentle with the devil. He needs to be driven out!

[Jesus said,] *"Now you understand that I have imparted to you all my authority to trample over his kingdom. You will trample upon every demon before you and overcome every power Satan possesses. Absolutely nothing will be able to harm you as you walk in this authority. However, your real source of joy isn't merely that these spirits submit to your authority, but that your names are written in the journals of heaven and that you belong to God's kingdom. This is the true source of your authority"* (Luke 10:19-20).

This portion of Scripture reveals things to help Christians move into their authority on earth. Christians must understand these truths so they can also understand the concepts that Jesus was discussing in Luke 10. These understandings will help Christians to walk in the truths that Jesus shared and help them to succeed in life.

Reading a verse only once or twice does not mean a person will fully understand the truth. Believers must meditate and think over these truths so that they develop a more complete understanding of the things that Jesus taught. Believers also must listen to people who teach those same truths. After thought, meditation, and receiving excellent teaching on these truths, people can start to acquire enough understanding that they will begin to see the manifestation of God's promises in their own lives. Jesus said that those who believe in Him, who are the believing ones, would have signs following. Those signs include healing the sick, raising the dead, and casting out devils. In His life here on earth, Jesus performed those very activities. However, many believers have never experienced seeing the healing of the sick, the raising of the dead, or the casting out of devils. To experience such things is a key to understanding the Kingdom authority that God has given to His sons and daughters here on the earth.

DISCERN THE AUTHORITY OF JESUS

Every believer must have a desire to discern the authority of Jesus. In order to discern His authority, Christians must first recognize that Jesus is King. Jesus has a Kingdom called *the Kingdom of God*, and He is in charge of that Kingdom. Jesus has all authority. He has the highest rule. His name is the strongest name. His name rules above all names. He, in His place of power, is above everyone and everything. Jesus said that believers are to speak in His name. That means that Jesus has issued an order to Christians. They are to trample on serpents and scorpions, and they are to drive out the devil. Then the effect of the believer's actions will have the same effect as if Jesus were on the earth doing those things.

Demons do not look at believers and become afraid just because of who they happen to be. The fear that demons possess starts with two facts: they know the One who sent the believer, and they know that Jesus is the supreme authority. God wants every believer to understand the ministry of Jesus. The Book of Acts explains His ministry, and God desires that Christians understand what that book reveals. It talks about how Jesus went around doing good and healing everyone who was oppressed of the devil (see Acts 10:38). Jesus went about healing; He did not place sickness upon anyone. Jesus was doing the will of His Father. The origin of all sickness, according to Scripture, is satan.

Jesus healed those who experienced oppression from the devil. This statement shows that the origin of sickness is the devil, not the Lord. Believers have the responsibility to drive out the devil, just as Jesus drove out the devil. Believers have the responsibility to heal the sick. Jesus drove out darkness wherever He went. Christians must begin to discern the authority of God. He has imparted that authority to them. They must begin to use that authority to go about doing good. Christians must place their faith in the person of Jesus Christ and His authority and power, and not place their faith in their own influence, power, or abilities.

FAITH AND AUTHORITY

Faith will cause a believer to move into the authority of God. Faith requires that a person discern Jesus. God's throne is fully established in Heaven. Everything that He does or says is true. If the Lord tells a person that they shall drive out devils, then they shall be able to drive out devils. The understanding of God's provision and finances requires an understanding of the power and purpose for which the

Lord has left believers here upon the earth. Jesus went about doing good, and that means He was a blessing to people everywhere He went. People had the opportunity to discern that Jesus actually was God's Son because of the great and mighty things that He did as He went about teaching, preaching, and healing the sick. If a person did not discern that He was God's Son, then Jesus was unable to help them in their need.

Jesus went to His hometown, and they did not discern Him as the Messiah. They recognized Jesus only as the carpenter's son, not as the Son of the Lord. Jesus Himself said, "I could not do many miracles there because of their unbelief." The people of His hometown saw Him only as a carpenter's son. They failed to discern that He was the son of David, the Messiah, or the Christ. Jesus was sent to earth as a Deliverer. When people cried out to Jesus as the Son of David, they got healed and delivered. However, when they discerned Jesus as merely Joseph's son, a carpenter's son, they did not receive anything. The Bible says He could not do anything except to heal a small number of minor ailments in the town where He grew up. He could heal only a few minor diseases in his hometown. His inability to do mighty miracles as He had performed elsewhere was a direct result of the fact that the people of His hometown did not discern Him as Jesus Christ the Messiah.

The person with the greatest faith Jesus ever encountered was not even a Jew. He was a Gentile, a Roman centurion. That centurion discerned authority, and Jesus recognized that his level of discernment meant that he was exercising great faith. Jesus knew that this man understood influence of authority and power well enough to ask a request and have great confidence and belief that Jesus would be able to deliver the answer. Therefore, Jesus also knew that this centurion actually understood the divine authority that

Jesus possessed. This man with great faith was not even in the covenant of the Jewish people. He was an outsider, a Gentile. Here is the story of the man of great faith, as told in the Book of Matthew:

> *As Jesus went into Capernaum, a centurion came up to Him, begging Him, and saying, Lord, my servant boy is lying at the house paralyzed and distressed with intense pains. And Jesus said to him, I will come and restore him. But the centurion replied to Him, Lord, I am not worthy or fit to have You come under my roof; but only speak the word, and my servant boy will be cured. For I also am a man subject to authority, with soldiers subject to me. And I say to one, Go, and he goes; and to another, Come, and he comes; and to my slave, Do this, and he does it. When Jesus heard him, He marveled and said to those who followed Him [who adhered steadfastly to Him, conforming to His example in living and, if need be, in dying also], I tell you truly, I have not found so much faith as this with anyone, even in Israel* (Matthew 8:5-10 AMPC).

Jesus has unbelievable power. His Word is enough to heal the sick. Jesus is the Commander of our faith, and He is the Commander of our life. Therefore, when Jesus gives a command to His people and He states something such as, "You are going to prosper," then that truly means that person will prosper. Other people who fail to have the right belief concerning prosperity are thinking incorrectly. Those who fail to believe that a person will prosper are incorrect. When the Lord has spoken that a person will prosper, he or she will prosper. Therefore, Christians must focus upon what the Lord has said rather than listen to those who fail to believe that

His Word is true. Other people often will try to convince people who are believing for great things that they are acting foolishly. Christians must focus upon what God has said and not listen to those who refuse to believe His promises.

The centurion displayed great faith. He even said that it was not necessary for Jesus to come to his house for His Word to work so that his servant could be healed. The centurion boldly declared that all that Jesus had to do was just say the word, and then the healing would be complete. Such belief in the authority of Jesus is completely accurate! Every time Jesus gives a command concerning deliverance for a person's life, that individual will be delivered. Every time Jesus says, "Receive your healing," then healing will definitely happen.

THE LORD IS WATCHING

The Lord is watching over His children and singing over them. In Zephaniah, it says:

> *The Lord your God is in your midst, a Warrior who saves. He will rejoice over you with joy; He will be quiet in His love [making no mention of your past sins], He will rejoice over you with shouts of joy* (Zephaniah 3:17 AMP).

The passage of Scripture clearly says that the Lord is a warrior who sings songs of deliverance over His children. He says that He is a Deliverer, and His Word is always true. Therefore, God freely gives every one of His own the absolute right to experience deliverance. However, a believer must sometimes stand on the Word of God and wait for the Lord to orchestrate that deliverance. The role that a Christian sometimes has to play in that deliverance is to wait patiently until that deliverance manifests. Sometimes it takes time for victory to manifest. The same thing can happen in the application of supernatural finances. A Christian may need to stand, believing the Lord, and wait patiently for solutions to financial situations. The Lord leads Christians into all good things and all truth. Believers may experience the same type of situation concerning His Word for financial blessings—they must stand upon the authority behind what the Lord says.

God does not want believers to be sick. He does not want believers to be in poverty. He wants Christians to have an abundance to meet the needs in their lives. Additionally, He wants Christians to have an abundance so they can give on any occasion, supplying the needs of others.

God is not going to leave His people sick, and He is not going to leave them destitute. Eventually, God will orchestrate everything so that His people will experience healing. God will deliver His own from poverty. He will cause them to prosper. The Lord has commanded Heaven's blessings to come to His children. Deuteronomy 28 reveals that people have but two choices in life—blessing or cursing. A person may choose to be above the curses upon the earth, or a person may choose to be beneath the curses upon the earth. There are but two choices, and every person on earth will select either choice. Deuteronomy makes this very clear—there are but two choices offered for mankind throughout the whole chapter.

Deuteronomy 28 reveals an important concept—the God of the Old Testament has not changed. He has not changed at all. He is the same yesterday, today, and forever. God, reveals Himself through Jesus Christ. Nothing has changed. The same promises that were in the Old Testament are also available in the New Testament.

Every believer can be a partaker of God's divine nature. In Second Peter, the apostle emphasizes this truth—all those who are born-again believers are able to be partakers of the divine nature. In order to partake of that divine nature, Christians must correctly implement the precious promises of God into their lifestyle. If believers will be faithful to implement those promises, they will be able to escape the corruption that is in the world. The lust for the things of the world will have no impelling power over Christians who will stand firm in faith upon God's Word. The good news is this: the Lord has shown believers how to implement the promises of God. Deuteronomy 28 reveals several things that a Christian needs to know to be able to achieve the abundant life that the Lord desires for each of His children:

> *All these blessings will come upon you and overtake you if you pay attention to the voice of the Lord your God. You will be blessed in the city, and you will be blessed in the field. The offspring of your body and the produce of your ground and the offspring of your animals, the offspring of your herd and the young of your flock will be blessed. Your basket and your kneading bowl will be blessed. You will be blessed when you come in and you will be blessed when you go out. The Lord will cause the enemies who rise up against you to be defeated before you; they will come out against you one way, but flee before you seven ways. The Lord will command the blessing upon you in your storehouses and in all that you undertake, and He will bless you in the land which the Lord your God gives you* (Deuteronomy 28:2-8 AMP).

Overcome with Blessings

The Lord has provided a way for every one of His children to overcome all challenges. When Christians recognize the way that God provides for them to move into His promises, it will change their thinking. A person must take these things that the Lord has spoken and implement them into action in life. Christians who will listen to the advice of the Lord concerning blessings and who begin to implement that advice into every area of life will have a key to overcoming all challenges. They will realize that the Lord is commanding blessings upon His children. The perception of the commanded blessings of God upon a person's life will motivate a believer to choose blessings, and in choosing blessings, each believer will move into the type of continual prosperity that God has for each of His own. Believers who choose blessings will be in good health, and their souls are going to prosper. Blessings shall come upon Christians who will choose them, and blessings will overtake them.

It is important to take note of the following truths concerning the blessings that come upon and overtake Christians:

1. Blessings will come upon and overtake Christians when they choose to obey the voice of the Lord our God. When believers will obey God's voice, blessings will definitely follow that obedience to the Lord. It is as simple as that!

2. There will be an increase in everything a Christian possesses. The increase of possessions will belong to the believer, and that increase of possessions will continually grow.

3. The Lord will cause any enemy who rises against one of His own to experience defeat. The believer will see that enemy experience defeat. The enemies of any Christian will run; those enemies are going to be defeated. What a fantastic promise God gives His children when He says our enemies will run and be defeated!

4. The Lord will command the blessing upon believers in their storehouses and in all that they may set their hand to do.

5. God will bless His children in the land which the Lord is giving to them.

Believers will receive a remarkable number of promises if they will take them to heart. When Christians permit the Spirit of God to ignite these precious promises and they start to proclaim those things, they will have a sense of authority about themselves. If Christians will allow the authority of God to come into their lives in a more significant way, they will begin to walk in the blessings of the Lord as never before that time!

Christians need to recognize that the blessings that they can receive, as listed in Deuteronomy 28, have to do with witnessing that the God of Israel is the God who rules and reigns above all gods. Christians who move into those blessings will become a witness to other nations that the Word of God is true, and that God is a God who blesses His own. They will create a testimony of His eternal goodness and power by their successful lives.

God blessed His children because He wanted to confirm His covenant with the people of Israel. In blessing Israel, God was able to display Himself to the other nations. Christians who have the favor of God on their lives should possess such prosperity and health that the people of the world are tempted to be jealous of their abundance. Christians who dare to believe that the favor of God will come upon them at the moment that they receive this good report will not be disappointed. God wants to change some incorrect perceptions that Christians possess so that He can cause revelation to come into their lives. The Holy Spirit will bring truth into the life of Christians, and they will become aware of any blind spots in their perceptions. The Lord will reveal incorrect ways of thinking so that Christians can change their mindsets and think in a new and different way. The new perceptions will help change their thoughts to make them effective. Christians who belong to God's family and Kingdom must know how to approach situations and problems correctly. The revelations that God gives His children will initiate a process that leads to success for all who will change their thoughts to coordinate with the way that the Lord wants them to think. When Christians come into line with what God says and what He intends for their lives, it is a priceless experience. Deuteronomy 28:11-13 promises these things:

> *The Lord will give you prosperity in the land he swore to your ancestors to give you, blessing you with many children, numerous livestock, and abundant crops. The Lord will send rain at the proper time from his rich treasury in the heavens and will bless all the work you do. You will lend to many nations, but you will never need to borrow from them. If you listen to these commands of the Lord your God that I am giving you today, and if you carefully obey them, the Lord will make you*

*the head and not the tail, and you will always be on top
and never at the bottom* (NLT).

This passage contains God's promises. First of all, none of His own will be in any debt, and second of all, every need in the lives of Christians will be met. There will be nothing lacking and nothing missing from a Christian's life. When a Christian matures in his or her thinking so it agrees with the Lord's Word, full abundance is possible.

Everyone around prosperous Christians is going to need what those successful Christians possess. Therefore, those Christians are going to be in demand. They will be able to help meet the needs of others. Christians will be so prosperous that they will be able to give and lend to people and never have to borrow from anyone. When Christians enter into this realm of abundance in life, then they have dominion. They will be an example of people who possesses complete authority in every aspect of life.

Those nations which have God on their side will be the wealthiest nations, and they will possess the most firepower. They will become the most powerful nations on earth. Although God is with a nation, that nation must still have resources to be in dominion so its people will be to be able to rule and reign upon this earth. God produced wealth in the nation of Israel through the principles that are found in Deuteronomy 28. God says that His children had the ability to choose blessings. This passage of Scripture was a testament for the nations surrounding Israel.

At this present time, this passage of Scripture is also a testament for any Christian who will receive the message found within it. Those who do not belong to the Lord will have to borrow, but anyone who serves the Lord will not have to borrow. Those who walk in this marvelous plan of the Lord are going to be the head, and they will be ones who are in command. Such supernatural prosperity will come to God's people that everyone who does not serve God will be afraid of those who belong to His Kingdom!

Although these truths are found in the Old Testament, they are just as relevant to Christians of today. They still apply to everyday life. The Holy Spirit will light up a godly path that is full of counsel for Christians. God wants His people to prosper as they progress in life. Christians should be the people who are lending money. Christians should not be the borrowers. It is important to get out of debt and break the power of poverty. Poverty in a Christian's life must be completely eradicated. The system of the world causes people to be in bondage. Satan uses the strategy of debt to entrap people.

Christians are the ones who should be the lenders to many nations. Believer must walk their way out of poverty. The Lord will lead believers who are knowledgeable, willing, and obedient to financial freedom when they take the authority God has freely provided and boldly address the enemy. God has ordained that Christians must break the devil's power and start to walk in freedom. Believers must continually meditate upon the Word of God. Victory is at hand when believers keep God's Holy Word before their eyes. It is wise for believers to ask God to help them find revelations for triumph in the areas of prosperity and wealth. Focusing upon God's ways produces victorious Christians!

Prayer

I am asking God to help us pass all of our money tests and transfer all the needed wealth into our hands right now so that we will have abundance to finance the work of the Gospel. We agree not only to be givers, but to allow the Lord to teach us how to be receivers as well. We say we will continually give, and we believe that this heavenly flow begins now. I say that we will see debt supernaturally disappear.

I speak God's blessing in our lives for ourselves and to help others who cannot help themselves. I ask that God will help those of us who are bound by debt to get free. Deuteronomy 29:9 says, "Therefore keep the words of this covenant, and do them, that you may prosper in all that you do." This is a covenant we have with You, God. We receive all the benefits of this covenant, in the name of Jesus.

As Christians, we have a blood covenant with God. God is the greater One in the covenant, and we decree that He is going to take us to His place of supernatural finances. Jesus is going to cause us to triumph over the world system. We are going to start to acquire supernatural finances so that we can do the work of God on the earth. We declare that God is performing supernatural miracles for us in our finances right now. God has given us the terms of the covenant and declared our part in the agreement. We agree that God will prosper us in order to confirm what He has promised through that covenant.

We allow the Holy Spirit to minister to us right now and set us free from all bondage of lack or bondage of being a victim. We speak against the problem of anyone who thinks that he or she can accept any lack or any victim mentality. We speak against any false ideas that we may have in saying we can manage lack or handle a victim mentality. We declare that freedom and financial prosperity come to us because we are willing to claim them right now!

We decree now that there is such a great overflow of supernatural finances that we will be well able to give to other people and help them. Deuteronomy 30:9 says, "The Lord your God will make you abound in all the work of your hand, in the fruit of your body, in the increase of your livestock, and in the produce of your land for good. For the Lord will again rejoice over you for good as He rejoiced over your fathers." We claim that promise in the Word as our own promise today.

We accept the truth that moving into supernatural finances and abundance involves the works of our hands. We acknowledge that our supernatural finances have to do with whatever we do for a living. We vow to let God into our finances and to allow the Lord to expand our revelation knowledge and actions so that we are prepared to move into supernatural abundance. We declare that there is such a great increase coming to us that we will have extreme abundance and be able to give to others. We declare that the finances will come forth to fund the sharing of the Gospel. We acknowledge that the message of the Gospel is free. We acknowledge that although the Gospel is free, the delivery system to get the message to people does require financial support.

We declare that we will be able to finance the preaching of the Gospel. We declare that we will bring in the tithe and offerings into the storehouse. We acknowledge that our gifts support the vision of doing God's work in the earth.

I came back from the heavenly realm. I did not want to come back, but I came back with a mission, a vision, and a job to do. I tell people all the time, "You do not have to give to me, and I do not want you to give to me. I want you to give to the vision and the work of the ministry that God sent me to do."

We acknowledge that a person who has the desire to partner with a ministry and their vision must be willing to give to God. We also acknowledge that there is no set requirement that the person give to a ministry with which they partner. We know it is important to give to God. We acknowledge that if a person agrees that the mission of a ministry is worthy of their support, then they should support it. We acknowledge that God calls us to go forth with authority. We acknowledge that, according to Deuteronomy 28, we have the ability to lend money to many nations, and we have the ability to never be in a situation where we must borrow. We declare that we will prosper in such abundance that we will be able to give and not have to borrow. We acknowledge that in these things, we stand in authority and power. We pray these things in the name of Jesus, knowing with full confidence that He will fulfill His part and answer our prayer.

Market Share

Big corporations have authority because they have the market share; they have a big chunk of the pie. When they control market share, then they have more authority to determine what actions they will take. Supernatural finances come into the Kingdom of God on this earth because money is essential to doing the work of the Lord upon this earth. Christians should never stop giving. When Christians give, they are expressing the authority that has been designated to them by their Father, the Lord. God gives Christians wealth, and He gives them authority as well. The wealth and authority that God gives to Christians are for the purpose of carrying forth His wishes on the earth.

God is trusting Christians to handle wealth in a righteous manner. God is in the business of training His children throughout their entire lives so that their actions will be righteous actions. Once the character of Christians reaches a mature level and they have attained a level where God is able to trust them, the Lord will trust them with great wealth. God will observe how people handle the wealth that comes, and at a certain point the Lord has confidence that they will not selfishly take the wealth that He gives all for themselves. When Christians have great wealth, then they have money to give to God's work, and His Kingdom will be able to spread throughout the whole earth. When all people have had the chance to hear the Good News, this present age will come to an end, and the Millennial reign of Christ will begin. Job 36:11 says, "If they obey and serve Him, they shall spend their days in prosperity and their years and pleasures."

Job mirrors a lot of the other language in other scriptures. People who obey and serve Him will spend their days in prosperity and their years in pleasures. When someone obeys, it is an act of service. Deuteronomy confirms that fact because the language of Deuteronomy matches the language of Job 36:11. The Holy Spirit reveals things about the lives of believers. In Proverbs, God says that believers should seek wisdom and should fear the Lord. Proverbs 3:1-2 says, "My son, do not forget my law, but let your heart keep my commands; for length of days and long life and peace they will add to you."

If believers keep the Word of God, they are going to have a long life. He is going to add peace to that long life. Christians are to act in mercy and truth and be led by mercy and truth. They are to write them on the tablet of their hearts, and they will find favor and high esteem in the sight of God and man.

The Lord is going a step further than just providing wealth for His own. He gives what is called "favor." The Word promises that Christians will find favor and high esteem in the sight of God and man. So, can a believer imagine being approved by God and man as well? Yes! Favor is all about the realm of influence. God can give His children great favor, which is actually a necessary part of authority. When believers have favor in this realm, that favor will cause believers to have significant influence. Influence with other people is part of authority. God wants to move His children into great favor.

The Lord wants Christians to encounter some things that will cause favor so they will prove that God is with them in front of the whole world. God desires to preach to the world through the great success of His own precious sons and daughters. God desires people to see that He is the only true God. He will be able to show that His people are evidence that He is the only true God when His children adjust their attitude toward Him. Christians must submit and yield to Him. They must allow that authority to help them to walk on this earth with great success, and then others can see evidence that God does exist and that He is with His children.

I remember the time that the Lord spoke to my wife and me to buy a violin for a young girl in our church. Shortly after we were spoken to by the Lord, I went to purchase a violin, and the Lord stopped me. He told me that I was not going to write a check for the violin but that it would cost me something besides that. He told me to fast two meals a day for the next nine months and purchase the violin with the money that I would've spent on my food. So, after nine months, I acquired enough money to buy the violin, and I presented it to her parents at church.

The father of the girl later told me that I hadn't realized what a miraculous thing I had done. I could see that he was deeply touched as he told me his side of the story. He said to me that every night he prayed with his children in their rooms before they went to bed. The frequent request of his daughter who received the instrument was that she wanted a violin from God. So, you can see that everything you do counts and the sacrifices you make could mean that you are the answer to someone else's prayer by your obedience.

Shortly after the violin encounter, the Lord told us to purchase a cello for a music minister in the church as well. When we announced it to him, he began to weep. The music minister played the violin but was believing that Jesus would give him a cello because they could not afford one. He rejoiced at the fact that the Lord knew even though he had not spoken of it and thanked my wife and me for our obedience to give it to him. This man was so encouraged, and he was able to play it very well for the Lord.

Chapter 11

THE WORD OF THE LORD AND SOWING AND REAPING

As for God, His way is perfect; the word of the Lord is proven; He is a shield to all who trust in Him (Psalm 18:30).

SPIRIT LIFE

In this chapter, I want to share with you the word of the Lord concerning sowing and reaping. This is an incredible chapter because the Lord has shown how He gives the word to us and then as we proceed forward with that word to fulfillment, it produces a harvest that automatically comes to us. God is so powerful; He cannot allow Himself to encounter mockery as the Scripture says:

Make no mistake about it; God will never be mocked! For what you plant will always be the very thing you harvest. The harvest you reap reveals the seed that was planted. If you plant the corrupt seeds of self-life into this natural realm, you can expect to experience a harvest of corruption. If you plant the good seeds of Spirit-life you will reap the beautiful fruits that grow from the everlasting life of the Spirit (Galatians 6:7-8 TPT).

There is a process of the word of the Lord coming forth and a person sowing and reaping the results of that word. A word from God initiates it, whether written or spoken, given from the heart of God and received by anyone who allows it to take firm root in the soil of their heart. The word of the Lord is coming forth strongly in these days. Many people are speaking by the Spirit. One of the things that is happening with the word of the Lord is that God is revealing the intent of His heart in a more significant way. The exciting thing is that we are starting to adopt His heart in the harvest. When we go forth, we have compassion, realizing that it is all about the lost people of this fallen world. We are beginning to see the importance of going out and testifying about Jesus.

In Psalm 18:30 it says, "As for God, His way is perfect; the word of the Lord is proven; He is a shield to all who trust in Him." This is the key verse for this chapter. We need to meditate on this truth that God's way is perfect. First of all, we have to establish the fact that God's ways are perfect. There is not a better way than His way. A lot of maturity needs to come in a believer's life in order to walk in supernatural finances. At the time of this writing I have been walking with the Lord now for thirty-nine years, and every day I learn something new. I know His voice more, but I also know His heart. I understand His personality in a more excellent way than I did when I first got saved. I have had to learn over the years that His way is a perfect way.

> Just recently I was shown greater revelation concerning supernatural finances.

There are times when believers think their way is better, but they are proven wrong. I got to the place where I don't waste any more time doing things any other way besides His way. Now, all the ministry that I passionately do on the earth, those things that I was sent back for, is to teach people how to do His will without delay. I now impart how to walk with God without having to go through the unnecessary burdens and hurts that we go through. Finding things out on our own is not the way to do it. It is time to tell people, "Listen, this is the proven way, and there is a short-cut. The shortcut is that God's way is perfect, and our way may not be." We desperately need to have the Word of the Lord. It is time to seek God and let the Spirit help us find a word in Scripture in order to hear from God in everything we do. We must obey what the Scripture says.

We must look into the Word of the Lord. Many times, God has spoken to us and told us to do certain things. We have to learn to obey instantly. Many times we find out that God is telling us to do our part by giving to others. A large part of a Christian's training concerning hearing God's voice is in the area of supernatural sowing. When a Christian is told to sow supernaturally into something or someone as God instructs them to, the act of planting can be the giving of goods or services. It can also involve our precious time as well. It does not have to always include money. It will consist of something a believer has that will cost him or her something and requires immediate obedience. This process is necessary because of the need to eliminate doubt and fear because the harvest on their sowing is dependent upon obedience to the Lord's proven Word.

When the word of the Lord comes to you, obey that word immediately and see your harvest.

CHEERFUL GIVING

I have learned not to question God as His heart toward us is perfect. He is a shield to all who trust Him, so He is going to protect us. We need to learn to trust Him more. In Second Corinthians, Paul says:

> *But this I say: He who sows sparingly will also reap sparingly, and he who sows bountifully will also reap bountifully. So let each one give as he purposes in his heart, not grudgingly or of necessity; for God loves a cheerful giver. And God is able to make all grace abound toward you, that you, always having all*

*sufficiency in all things, may have an abundance for
every good work* (2 Corinthians 9:6-8).

The apostle Paul had authority over the churches as an apostle of the Church of Jesus Christ. He would address many issues, including finances. In this passage of Scripture, he discusses the area of offerings. Paul is talking about finances in the context of chapter nine, specifically offerings as they pertain to sowing and reaping. Paul is giving them instructions on giving and receiving as well. He is laying out some groundwork on how to sow according to what a person would want to receive—that is the way he explains it here. Paul says that when a Christian sows sparingly or little, they will reap little. It is just a natural law. Conversely, when you sow bountifully, you reap bountifully. Paul is talking to the Corinthians about money here in this context as it relates to offerings; so let each one as they purpose in their heart not give grudgingly.

We should never do anything out of a wrong attitude in our heart or because of pressure.

Paul also says not to give out of necessity either. However, He says if a person holds back, then their harvest will be small. But if a person does not hold back and gives abundantly, then their yields will be abundant! Then Paul tells us that we are not under compulsion or forced to do anything. Paul genuinely allows a person to choose his or her own free will.

We should never do anything out of a wrong attitude in our heart or because of pressure. We should do it because we have purposed in our heart that it's what we want to do. God loves a cheerful giver, and this is the conclusion that Paul offers here.

However, the next statement is a very crucial point here as well. "God is able to make all grace abound toward you." Paul says that the supernatural result of not sowing grudgingly or sparingly, but giving because we want to and abundantly, is that God can abound toward us through His grace. We will always have sufficiency in all things; we will have an abundance of provision. That *abundance* is in every good work. God is going to supply all of our needs.

Supernatural finances are going to come at us like a wave of abundance so that we can give on every occasion. God sincerely wants to bless His people. The Holy Spirit is saying, "It is up to you, but if I were you I would go ahead and not hold back." This is what God is saying here.

We have to remember that we can do what we desire when it comes to giving. However, we should look at what Paul is saying in its context. Paul is talking about finances and giving in Second Corinthians 9, and so he is saying that we should not hold back. We should give according to our faith, but we should also keep in mind that God is not going to fail us. He is going to keep track of everything we do.

REAPING IN DUE SEASON

And let us not grow weary while doing good [sowing],
for in due season we shall reap if we do not lose heart
(Galatians 6:9).

In Galatians 6 it says to not grow weary while doing good. In this case, don't grow weary at the idea of sowing, for in due season we will reap if we do not lose heart. The principle here is that we sow and then we reap, but we do not grow weary when we plant and wait for the harvest.

> *So now, brethren, I commend you to God and to the word of His grace, which is able to build you up and give you an inheritance among all those who are sanctified* (Acts 20:32).

Paul is encouraging people in the Book of Acts that the word of God's grace can build us up and give us an inheritance among all those who are saying that there is an eternal purpose to everything we do.

 So really, nothing is ever lost. Whatever a person does not obtain in this life they will gain in the next. Everything is kept track of in Heaven.

THE WORD PROSPERS

> *So shall My word be that goes forth from My mouth; it shall not return to Me void, but it shall accomplish what I please, and it shall prosper in the thing for which I sent it* (Isaiah 55:11).

The Lord is adamant about His Word. Whatever goes forth from His mouth will not come back to Him without accomplishing whatever He has desired. God said His Word would prosper in the thing that it was sent it to do. God speaks forth what He knows and desires, and it is going to come back doing precisely what He said it would. That is the absolute truth about this Scripture.

When a person reaps a harvest of something, it is because they sowed something. It is the law of cause and effect at work. The whole reason a person sows is that they want to reap a harvest. A person would not sow unless they wanted to reap a harvest. It is the same with God. He would not speak a word unless He expected it to come to pass. So, He only speaks those things which He wants to come to pass because everything He says comes to pass!

> When you sow, you reap, because God has already set it in motion. It must bring back a harvest.

God will watch over that harvest and we will gain from our giving. That is the way it is set up. Everything that's in a seed produces itself. So, when you plant the seed, it comes back with the same thing but in a more significant measure.

God wants to honor His word. He's already shown us through this study that He wants to prosper us. It's really not a question anymore. However, there are some things that you can do personally to become better soil. Did you know that Jesus spoke in Matthew 13 about this?

ARE YOU GOOD SOIL?

When we reveal, implement, and practice our covenant with the Lord Jesus Christ in our lives, then we become attractive to Heaven. If Heaven is for you, then you must accept this as a fact. We must be people who are led by the Spirit of God so that we are able to have the Kingdom of God begin to work in our lives. If only we would allow the Holy Spirit to communicate this to us, we would do so much better.

On one occasion, Jesus spoke with me about the parable of the sower. I was shocked at how much I did not understand about this parable. After seeking God, I realized that this parable is concentrating on the condition of the soil and should be referred to as the *parable of the soil* instead. Let's look deeply into what Jesus taught in this parable. But before we do this, I would like to quote what Jesus said about this parable, translated from the Aramaic language, which He spoke fluently:

> *"If you're able to understand this, then you need to respond."* *Then his disciples approached Jesus and asked, "Why do you always speak to people in these hard-to-understand parables?"* *He explained,* ***"You've been given the intimate experience of insight into the hidden truths and mysteries of the reign of heaven's kingdom****, but they have not. For everyone who listens with an open heart will receive progressively more revelation until he has more than enough. But those who don't listen with an open, teachable heart, even the understanding that they think they have will be taken from them"* (Matthew 13:9-12 TPT).

Wow, I can just hear Jesus saying this! I can hear Him letting us know that He wants us to meditate on His words until those words become so much a part of us that what He says influences every aspect of our lives. "You've been given the *intimate experience of insight* into the *hidden truths* and *mysteries* of the *reign of heaven's kingdom!*" The Spirit of God seeks out the deep things of God.

> But God has revealed them to us through His Spirit.
> For the Spirit searches all things, yes, the deep things of
> God (1 Corinthians 2:10).

I want to know the deep things of God. Jesus said that if we understand the parable of the sower, we have been given the deep, intimate, hidden truths and mysteries of the Kingdom of Heaven. Because we understand that God offers us such great understanding of His truths, we must respond.

> I have to share these truths with you because you are going to be effective in prayer and supernatural finances. You can get every prayer answered when you fully understand what I am explaining.

> Then He spoke many things to them in parables, saying: "Behold, a sower went out to sow. And as he sowed, some seed fell by the wayside; and the birds came and devoured them. Some fell on stony places, where they did not have much earth; and they immediately sprang up because they had no depth of earth. But when

the sun was up they were scorched, and because they had no root they withered away. And some fell among thorns, and the thorns sprang up and choked them. But others fell on good ground and yielded a crop: some a hundredfold, some sixty, some thirty. He who has ears to hear, let him hear!" And the disciples came and said to Him, "Why do You speak to them in parables?" He answered and said to them, "Because it has been given to you to know the mysteries of the kingdom of heaven, but to them it has not been given. For whoever has, to him more will be given, and he will have abundance; but whoever does not have, even what he has will be taken away from him. Therefore I speak to them in parables, because seeing they do not see, and hearing they do not hear, nor do they understand. And in them the prophecy of Isaiah is fulfilled, which says: 'Hearing you will hear and shall not understand, and seeing you will see and not perceive; for the hearts of this people have grown dull. Their ears are hard of hearing, and their eyes they have closed, lest they should see with their eyes and hear with their ears, lest they should understand with their hearts and turn, so that I should heal them'" (Matthew 13:3-15).

Here is where we must receive the Spirit of revelation that Paul talked about in the book of Ephesians:

That the God of our Lord Jesus Christ, the Father of glory, may give to you the spirit of wisdom and revelation in the knowledge of Him, the eyes of your understanding being enlightened (Ephesians 1:17-18).

 Lord, we desire to have eyes that see and ears that hear. We are listening to what the Holy Spirit is saying to us about these truths in our life! Amen.

Listen as Jesus explains these truths to us. Remember that we must have "eyes that see and ears that hear."

But blessed are your eyes, because they see; and your ears, because they hear. I tell you the truth, many prophets and righteous people longed to see what you see, but they didn't see it. And they longed to hear what you hear, but they didn't hear it.

Now listen to the explanation of the parable about the farmer planting seeds: The seed that fell on the footpath represents those who hear the message about the Kingdom and don't understand it. Then the evil one comes and snatches away the seed that was planted in their hearts. The seed on the rocky soil represents those who hear the message and immediately receive it with joy. But since they don't have deep roots, they don't last long. They fall away as soon as they have problems or are persecuted for believing God's word. The seed that fell among the thorns represents those who hear God's word, but all too quickly the message is crowded out by the worries of this life and the lure of wealth, so no fruit is produced. The seed that fell on good soil represents those who truly hear and understand God's word and produce a harvest of thirty, sixty, or even a hundred times as much as had been planted! (Matthew 13:16-23 NLT)

1. The Sower: A farmer who plants seeds. *Webster's Dictionary, 1828 Edition* defines a *sower* as "he that scatters seed for propagation. One who scatters or spreads; as a sower of words."

2. The Seed: The seed is the Word. According to Webster's, a *seed* is "the substance, animal or vegetable, which nature prepares for the reproduction and conservation of the species. The seeds of plants are a deciduous part, containing the rudiments of a new vegetable."

3. The Ground: Webster defined *ground* as "the surface of land or upper part of the earth, without reference to the materials which compose it." In this parable, there are four types of soil. Jesus explained that these soil conditions are four possible conditions of a man's heart.

FOUR CONDITIONS OF A PERSON'S HEART

The Hard Heart

It is imperative to not only hear what God is saying but understand it as well. Jesus, in person, wanted me to grasp the truth that is taught. He wanted me to take truth into my heart so that it produced a crop. Remember, it is possible for someone to hear but walk away *not understanding* what they just heard. Do not let the evil one come and *snatch away* the Word that is planted in your heart.

The Rocky Heart

We all have had the experience of hearing the Word of God and encountering such an awesome joy. We need to make sure that we have a depth concerning our walk with God. Our commitment level will determine our longevity during *troubles*. When we encounter *persecution* for believing God's Word, we will not relinquish our joy and produce a crop.

What is the Holy Spirit saying to you about the soil of your heart? Let's pray about it now: We ask You, Lord, to prepare our soil as we give our hearts completely to You! Amen.

The Thorny Heart

Many of us are very busy with the affairs of this life on earth. We must not allow the Word to be crowded out by the *worries* of this life and the *attraction of wealth*. The thorns are pushing out the truth of the Kingdom in your soil.

The Good Heart

The good soil is the heart that genuinely receives and understands what God is saying and produces an exceptional harvest, even a hundred times as much as had been planted!

One of the most exciting characteristics of Jesus is this: He is so simple in His approach toward truth. He gave us a sincere way to understand the way that the Kingdom of Heaven works. It is interesting to note that there is nothing to be done with the seed except to sow it.

The farmer sows the seed. That is what farmers do. The Lord Jesus instructed me that the seed has everything within it and is missing nothing essential to growth. A seed contains within itself all that is necessary for propagation. Once planted, it sprouts and produces a crop. Keep this in mind—one does not have to do anything else but just plant, water, and wait.

THE WORD OF THE LORD

Every time I am speaking at a conference, I begin to minister on certain subjects concerning people's hearts through the word of knowledge. I am actually ministering to their soil, which may contain rocks and thorns and other hindrances that prevent the soil's production of the Word that is sown. The Lord showed me how to deal with the soil first, getting it ready for the sowing of the Word by ministering to the people through the word of knowledge, word of wisdom, discerning of spirits, and prophecy. He told me that if I did this, I would see a greater harvest when I sowed the Word during those times that I am teaching.

The process may take ten minutes or an hour. To most people, it may seem as if I am randomly talking, but what I am really doing is getting rid of any hindrances in those who are listening so that the Word of God takes root and produces a crop in those individuals. Jesus comes and stands beside me and tells me what is in the hearts of people. Once I know the conditions that exist, I will start to speak out on certain subjects and minister to the people as a body or individually, however God so chooses. After the Lord takes care of the issues with the people's soil, the glory will come in as I minister the Word to the people. He also tells me to speak to the staff of the church or ministry separately in a closed session. He will tell me at times to speak to the intercessory prayer group and the worship group as well in a closed session. He told me that if I could get the leadership on the same page as Him, the rest of the church or ministry would follow.

We have things that are bothering us. I know that we do not want to be that way but it sometimes gets overwhelming. But if we yield to the Holy Spirit, He can start to set people free. The Lord of the breakthrough desires to break His people out.

> So David went to Baal-perazim and defeated the Philistines there. "The Lord did it!" David exclaimed. "He burst through my enemies like a raging flood!" So he named that place Baal-perazim (which means "the Lord who bursts through)" (2 Samuel 5:20 NLT).

We can receive the Word of God with greater ease when we are relieved of those things that have bothered us. So, if there is a confirming word that can be spoken, then we should do that because it frees up the people to receive the message of the Lord and then they are not thinking about their problems.

The Lord showed me that every encounter involving ministry to someone should involve people encountering freedom. Ministry of the Spirit is breaking the powers of darkness off people and setting them free, speaking words of wisdom, words of knowledge about their future, prophesying, and continually sowing good seed into people's lives.

However, at the same time we must be mindful that even people who seem to be doing well have things going on in their lives. That is why we have to yield to the word of wisdom, word of knowledge, and prophecy to speak to people on a spiritual level so that they can experience release. Many people will not be able to listen to what you have to say because of what they are going through. To a person who is struggling, their problems are so much more significant than what you are teaching. They are asking God, "Why am I going through what I am going through?" When there is supernatural ministry time given, people will be touched supernaturally, and then they can listen and receive the Word.

SUPERNATURAL SOWING

There is the sowing of our physical riches in faith that provides for the entrance into supernatural finances. When a person plants in obedience to the voice of the Spirit, they are going to reap the Holy Spirit's reward for that obedience. Simply put, the seed produces a crop after its kind. So, whatever it is that a person has sown, it then produces after its kind. If you are giving out of a right heart, you then understand sowing into the Kingdom. Jesus said if you understand this parable of the sower, you understand the whole Kingdom. Christians need to understand that the Kingdom of God does involve finances in this physical realm. Supernatural finances involve the transference of wealth in the physical realm between people because there is not any money in Heaven.

Down here in the earthly physical realm, the Kingdom of God is advancing, but He needs people who will be His hands and feet. The finances are here on the earth, but they become supernatural when dedicated to God. He can show you where to put your finances so that they are the most effective for His use. You can invest in places where God will get a good return on the finances you gave into His work. When you give, you can give supernaturally into the soil God tells you to put into because He wants you to sow toward a particular harvest. So, everybody has a field. Some people water in that field, some people plant, but God gives the increase according to what Paul said.

Trust in God that He is tending to the soil in your heart and that you are receiving a big harvest from the Word of God. In our life, there is a transfer of the principle of sowing into good soil. You are going to reap a crop if you sow into a ministry of someone who is doing the work of God. You can expect to get out of that a return or harvest because there are people who are going to hear the gospel because you sowed into ministers financially.

SUPERNATURAL SEED

Jesus's teaching on the parable of the sower ties in with supernatural finances and giving with the whole principle of the seed. The truth of the matter is that the seed is not money according to Jesus. Jesus said the seed was the Word of God. However, in the Word of God, you can find all these things that we have been studying about supernatural finances—biblical prosperity, wealth, giving and receiving, and warfare with this system of debt in this physical realm. To be a Christian and to give finances away is the exact opposite of what the world system stands for under lucifer's rule.

However, the Word also teaches us many other subjects that are part of the seed of the Word. There is healing, righteousness, holiness, and the gifts of the Spirit that are all part of the Word that we can receive a crop on.

So, there is the principle that when you sow in the good soil, you are going to get a return back as it pertains to the Kingdom of God. One of the principles in the Word of God is giving; another is receiving. And through this principle, God brings to us prosperity and increase. Part of giving is the fact that we will receive a harvest back because this is a true principle. We need to focus on what God is saying to us so that when we give, we give in the right place because we have been destined to do certain things in this life that God has written in our book in Heaven (see Ps. 139:16).

Just believe that even the finances we earned in this life are predestined for a particular assignment. So, there are finances designated for different needs around you. However, there are also finances that are designated to be sown into a field in a foreign country through a missionary or a ministry who is doing the will of God there. That money is earmarked for that. You will have to pray that God shows you precisely what to do because this is all supernatural.

I recall a time when I wanted to discern God's will and could not get clarity. It concerned some leadership training that I was asked to attend at my church. It would require me to miss work. That meant the time for the leadership training would cost me a whole week's wages because it involved a long weekend. My job required me to travel, and I worked on an airplane for three days at a time, so I would have to lose the whole three-day trip. I remember entering an elevator at the hotel in Pittsburgh, Pennsylvania and asking the Lord again what I should do. I had asked the Lord for the answer to this same question several weeks prior with no response. This time, I stated my case and felt that I should at least have the conference paid by the church because I was losing a week's wages to attend the required training. I received no answer to my prayer, so I continued to my room and flew out the next day to complete my work week at the airline.

The next week I was in the very same hotel. As I stepped into the elevator, I realized that God had not yet answered. So, I stated my case again, including the fact that He should compensate me for the cost of the conference, which was a little over a hundred dollars. As I got off the elevator, I still did not hear Him say anything. I got my key out, placed it in the door, and entered my room for the night. Immediately, I heard the audible voice of God. He told me to get on my knees quickly. I thought I was in trouble, so I started to repent. *I am sorry for complaining, Lord*, I said. In an audible voice, He said, "Look under your bed." There, under my bed, was a one-hundred-dollar bill. There was a great deal of garbage under there also. The hundred-dollar bill was very old. However, I began to thank God for it and asked Him if I should change it into smaller denominations such as twenty-dollar bills because it looked so old and did not seem authentic to me. He told me it was real, and I put in my pocket.

The next morning as I was boarding my flight, a gentleman who was carrying a firearm with the proper paperwork checked in with me. This was the appropriate procedure for all armed individuals on an aircraft. He was with the Department of the Treasury counterfeit division. I saw that the Lord was providing me with the confirmation I needed concerning my one-hundred-dollar bill, so I pulled the bill out of my pocket and showed it to him. He said that it was old, but it was authentic. God had answered my prayer, and the gentleman went and sat down in his seat. God had confirmed to me His will. He provided the needed money and a confirmation of the authenticity of the one-hundred-dollar bill. I use this story as an example of the fact that God does answer our prayers and that we also must be specific with Him. The Holy Spirit will give us revelation on how to pray.

God's Kingdom finances are not a system that a Christian manipulates. These principles are truly what the Word of God teaches. Jesus said that when a person tends to their soil and they get healed, they can expect to receive a harvest back.

God will reward you for all your gifts.
He keeps track, so do not worry.

CONCLUSION

THE LORD HIMSELF DESIRES FOR YOU TO FINISH YOUR DEStiny according to what He has written about you beforehand in the books of Heaven. He will not ask you to fulfill something and then not make provision for it. You, as a dearly loved child of His, have a rich heritage in the family of God. Never doubt how important you are to Him and expect the provision to come from Heaven into your situation as you walk with Him. This life may not always be easy but it sure is rewarding when you do it *God's way*.

> Now is the time to do what your books in Heaven say, and supernatural finances are on the way!

ABOUT DR. KEVIN ZADAI

Kevin Zadai, Th.D. was called to ministry at the age of ten. He attended Central Bible College in Springfield, Missouri, where he received a Bachelor of Arts in theology. Later, he received training in missions at Rhema Bible College. He is currently ordained through Rev. Dr. Jesse and Rev. Dr. Cathy Duplantis. At age thirty-one, during a routine day surgery, he found himself on the "other side of the veil" with Jesus. For forty-five minutes, the Master revealed spiritual truths before returning him to his body and assigning him to a supernatural ministry. Kevin holds a commercial pilot license and is retired from Southwest Airlines after twenty-nine years as a flight attendant. He and his lovely wife, Kathi, reside in New Orleans, Louisiana.

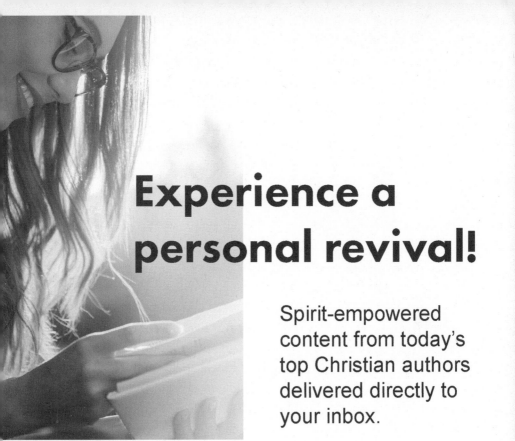